I ONLY HAVE AN HOUR

A Look at Mississippi through the Lens of a Black College Football Cultural Framework

Samuel L. Polk, Jr.

Sam weaves together a narrative of personal experience and integrates a strand of historical, powerful, and provocative stories to provide a glimpse of another side of Mississippi

> - Dr. J. Kenyatte Cavil, author of The State of Intercollegiate Athletics at HBCUs: Past, Present & Persistence and editor of The Athletic Experience at HBCUs: Past, Present, and Persistence

I Only Have An Hour is a fantastic read that provides a vivid account of Mississippi folklore. Sam Polk, Jr. conjures up the spirits of the past to reckon with Mississippi's current state of affairs. There is no one more passionate about preserving and illuminating Black History than Sam. He is an oracle on the watch to ensure the next generation is inspired to keep the ancestor's eternal candle bright.

> - Carlos A. Lock, author of *Black College Football: The Game That Time Forgot*

Sam Polk, Jr. is a scholar of the highest order, so much so it has cause me to address him as the "Minister of Information." As an educator, I look for works that not only give the history of what happened but a personal experience that relates to the information. Sam has done just that with *I Only Have An Hour*. The canon of Mississippi literature has gotten a new drum major.

> - Carlton Brandon Adkins, M.Ed.

1

Sam is one of the most prolific and fact-based storytellers of all time! He has an innate ability to consistently link obscure and seemingly unrelated points in history, much like a scattergram, to tell an engaging story in his very unique style.

- Spencer Rollins, MBA

Growing up in Jackson meant the SWAC was mine to love unashamed, to treat my guys in my conference like they were Hershel, Bo, or Dan Marino. You can have Touchdown Jesus, Between the Hedges, or Happy Valley. I had the Vet and way too many memories of Jackson State wins, losses, and one of the happiest football childhoods ever.

- Charles Bishop, of THEE PRE-GAME SHOW & INSIDE THE HBCU SPORTS LAB

Sam Polk, Jr. isn't simply a product of Black College Football; he's a product of Black dignity. That spiritual DNA specifically continues to influence the developmental character within its many coaches and players. Sam writes from this experiential lens bringing readers closer to the sweat, blood, and tears that laid the pastimes.

- Vincent E. H Joplin, Lead Pastor, and Founder, Delivering Word Bible Church, Memphis, TN

I played football with Sam at Lane College, a small HBCU in Jackson, TN. He was always a source of history for our people. One day we were bored in the dorm, and Sam said, "Hey bruh, let's roll." I had no idea where we were going to hang out. We ended up in Memphis, TN, at another small HBCU, LeMoyne-Owen College. He knew everyone there. He knew when the school was founded and its purpose for existence. Then, off to the Lorraine Motel, the site of the assassination of Dr. King. It was my first time seeing it in person. Rolling with Sam has always been an adventure. Brother Polk is a walking history lesson.

- Will Brown, CEO of Brown Brothers Entertainment

This volume is dedicated to my mother, Vivian Jean Polk, my father, Dr. Samuel L. Polk, Sr. my sister Xanshunta Polk, my wife Shamekka Polk, and my children Malia Ann Polk and Samuel L   Polk, III.

This volume is also dedicated to anyone who has ever attended a Black College football game in the state of Mississippi and to anyone who has attended a Black College football game throughout the HBCU sports diaspora.

TABLE OF CONTENTS

FOREWORD

The Southwestern Athletic Conference (SWAC) has just commemorated 100-years of athletic and academic history. The SWAC was formed on September 10, 1920, in Houston from humble beginnings as a grand experiment with five historically Black colleges and universities (HBCUs) member institutions (four private institutions and one public institution). The founding member institutions of the SWAC included Bishop College (now defunct) (1920-1956); Paul Quinn College, (1920-1929); Samuel Huston College (now Huston-Tillotson University), (1920-1959); and Wiley College (1920-1968) as well as one public institution, Prairie View State Normal & Industrial College (now Prairie View A&M University), (1920-Present) in the Southwest region of the United States with a sixth joining just a year later, Texas College (1921-1961).

While the Great Migration saw the forced exodus of six million African Americans seeking to escape the Southern American apartheid and move to the urban Northeast, Midwest, and West regions and into metropolitan cities between 1916 and 1970, the SWAC moved to the Southeast with the expansion of public HBCUs; Langston (1931-1957), Southern (1934-Present), Arkansas AM&N/Arkansas at Pine Bluff (1936-1970 / 1997-Present), Texas Southern (1954-Present), Grambling State (1958-Present), Jackson State (1958-Present), Alcorn State (1962-Present), and Mississippi Valley State (1968-Present). However, the SWAC continued its expansion further east via Alabama State (1982-Present) as well as Alabama A&M (1999-Present) and most recently with Florida A&M (1921-Present) and Bethune-Cookman

(1921-Present) to create the SWAC components of the HBCU sports culture and sporting HBCU diaspora.

The HBCU sports culture includes music as a participatory function of bands (i.e., the marching sport), cheerleaders (i.e., cheer and dance competitions), and sororities and fraternities (i.e., step-show competitions) as well as HBCU athletic events such as classics (i.e., football and basketball games) which include homecoming festivities, tailgating, and expos. The sporting HBCU diaspora framework embodies the Pan-Africanism context and, as such, is a composite of the long-storied historical extension of the African diaspora in the Americas and the culture illuminated throughout the African American community. Thus, as an integral part of the Black community, this book explores how activism operated in Mississippi, the SWAC, and specifically narrating this experience through the HBCU sports culture and HBCU athletic aesthetics.

Sam weaves together a narrative of personal experience and integrates a strand of historical, powerful, and provocative stories to provide a glimpse of another side of Mississippi.

Dr. J Kenyatta Cavil

Author of The State of Intercollegiate Athletics at HBCUs: Past, Present, & Persistence   and

Editor of The Athletic Experience at HBCUs: Past, Present, & Persistence

To grow in Jackson, MS, was a surreal experience. Jackson is the quintessential SWAC city. Located centrally within the conference with residents representing almost every school within the SWAC. You cannot help but be immerse in all things SWAC. Understand that barbershop conversations had nothing to do with Old Miss, Miss. State, or USM. It had everything to do with W.C., "Big John," "The Godfather," "The Gunslinger," and "Big Daddy."

To grow up in Jackson meant I witnessed firsthand Jerry Rice run the most perfect post pattern, Ike Holt crouch in his DB stance, a Willie Totten spiral, Lewis Tillman dotting the I, the '87 Jackson State linebackers (Lloyd, Conners, Conners, and Collins) and McNair improvise.

Growing up in Jackson meant the hair standing upon my neck hearing the opening bars of "Get Ready" from the JSU tubas, the Sounds of Dynamite, and "Supa Soul" and the best fight song in college football MVSU's "Devils Gun."

Growing up in Jackson meant the SWAC was mine to love unashamedly, to treat my guys to conferences like they were Hershel, Bo, or Dan Marino. You can have Touchdown Jesus, Between the Hedges, or Happy Valley. I had the Vet and way too many memories of Jackson State wins, losses, and one of the happiest football childhoods ever.

- Charles Bishop, of THEE PRE-GAME SHOW &
INSIDE THE HBCU SPORTS LAB

CHAPTER 1

CONCEPTUAL AND CONTEXTUAL FRAMING

> *"Never forget that intelligence rules the world and ignorance carries the burden. Therefore, remove yourself as far as possible from ignorance and seek as far as possible to be intelligent."*
>
> - Marcus Garvey

I am an African-centered thinker. I believe in the theoretical and genealogical concept of the African diaspora. This is a concept that is not only a thought concept or process for me but also a way of life. Malcolm X once famously stated with a brilliant analogy that "If a pregnant cat crawled in an oven and had babies, they aren't biscuits." Meaning that simply because born in an oven, the cat's offspring are still kittens no matter where they were born. This is because regardless of birthplace, the new offspring are kittens because their mother is a cat, and so are all of their ancestors before the mother.

The African diaspora is defined as anywhere Black people may be dispersed on the planet earth. Africa being our ancestral home, we are still Africans. We, as Black people, have been forced to hate all things African by design, and as a result, many of us hate our natural hair, African features and have throughout our sojourn in the western hemisphere tried to distance ourselves from our mother continent. This is a state of mind I have made my mission in life to combat.

I learned my life's mission at an early age. That mission is to educate myself as much as I can about the greatness of my peoples' past and as much about African Americans as I can in order to arm myself against the worthy opponent of white supremacy, which comes in many forms. Arguably, the most effective form, being misinformation about the lack of African contributions to humanity. I have researched, studied the history of my people not only so I can combat white supremacy in academia but also so I can combat the ignorance that lives among Black people about their own greatness. I have studied and researched for thirty years and tried to educate and inform as many as I can in many ways.

My first job out of college was as a beat writer for an all-black newspaper called the Metro Forum. 'Til this day, this was the most enjoyable work experience that I have ever had. I learned how to write under pressure and always work to be ahead of the competition. I also learned how to communicate eye to brain as opposed to ear to brain, which is a delicate skill set of its own. After working very hard writing pertinent and relevant stories concerning the local Black community, I had earned my own opinion-editorial column, and I was able to express my own thoughts in a very Pro-Black manner. This shocked the local community in ways that I had not expected. Some hated it and voiced their opinions with hate mail and death threats. Others voiced love for my writings and support for my ideas that had gained lots of attention.

Nevertheless, I also learned that the bottom line was the all mighty bottom dollar and that I could not voice my true thoughts of Black self-determination using the equipment of others. This book is my attempt to express some of those thoughts and stories in my way, this time in book form where I am in full control and have no one to answer or justify my topics' worthiness. However, that early writing experience as a young newspaperman was invaluable.

I have the privilege and honor of hosting my own podcast along with my friend of over twenty-five years Comedian Just Will (Will Brown). This podcast gives me the opportunity to discuss the African Diaspora and relevant issues with people, namely Black people, on a weekly basis, with a pretty large listening audience via platforms such as iheartradio, Spotify, Spreaker, and Facebook. Each subject or topic that I pick to discuss the following week becomes my baby. I study it, research it, care for it, feed it, nurture it, and put it to bed at night. The process starts on Wednesday night following the show. I pick my new topic, and for six days, I repeat the before mentioned parental duties with that subject. This arms me with a good knowledge base to attack the microphones with powerful and enlightening discourse. On Wednesday, it's showtime, and I am like a proud parent sending my now matured baby into the world to do its job of empowering the African Diaspora via the airways. However, as successful as I may be expounding on that topic, I cannot seem to fight off a weekly feeling of failure at the end of each episode.

See, I have a tendency to be long-winded. I am reminded almost weekly by my co-host that "time is about up my brother." Studying and researching as aggressively as I do, I only scratch the surface of the information I wanted to share with the people. I usually feel a desire to apologize for that fact. The apology ends up sounding like this at the conclusion of each week's episode, "Damn, I only have an hour, but for an hour, I'm gonna give you all I got." The podcast's hour length betrays me every time. This is where the title of this humble book got its origin. The same with an hour lecture or speaking engagement, no matter the amount of positive feedback I get, and I humbly receive plenty, I'm still disappointed in myself, a gift and a cure. Doing this work for so long, in fact, for all of my adult life, my reward comes in many forms. The best of which comes in the form of verbal and written feedback. I hear "you inspired me to read more," "I have read every book written by John G. Jackson because your discussion on him inspired me," and "you make me so proud to be Black or so proud to be of African descent" many times with a tear in their eye or even a teary heartfelt story that profoundly touches my soul.

On the contrary, I sometimes get feedback that forces me to fight my tears until I can get out of public view. For instance, there was the time I gave a talk at a local community center about Africa, and a youngster no older than twelve years of age looking at the cover of a book I had on the table asked me, "Is that Florida? Because that is where I'm from, Florida." That crushed me and almost overwhelmed me, but I held it together, and it made me stronger as I explained to the young man what he was looking at. This exchange caused the tears of others that watched. The latter sort of feedback, believe it or not, is more common, and it serves as a constant reminder that there is still massive amounts of work to do. That is why I take this mission so seriously. I allow nothing or no one to disturb me on my post. You don't have to agree with or even like me but get in my way or become a hindrance, and that's a declaration of war—zero Tolerance.

This volume is an ode to all of the men and women that have shaped my thinking into the African paradigm. African-centered scholars, thinkers, sociologists, and writers. Great men and women that have produced books that have been my lifelong companions and friends. Women such as Ida B. Wells, Frances Cress Welsing, Joy Degruy, and Gwen Ifill. Men such as members of the Harlem History club started in the 1930s based at the Harlem YMCA. Men like Nnamdi Azikwe who came to the states for an HBCU education and later became the President of Nigeria. Men like Kwame Nkrumah who also came to the United States for an HBCU education and later became the President of Ghana. Men like Richard B. Moore who warned us about the evil uses of the word Negro. Men like John Henrik Clarke, the most profound in the group in my humble opinion, who called The Harlem History Club "His first University." John G. Jackson, Willis Nathaniel Huggins, who owned Blyden Bookstore in Harlem. William Leo Hansberry, who was in Lorman, MS, and whose father was a professor at then Alcorn A&M College. Herbert Harrison and my favorite historian of all time J.A. Rogers, a Pullman Porter who on every stop of the train found a bookstore or library in order to research, study and collect our history.

Arthur A. Schomburg, the great Afro-Puerto Rican researcher, collector, and bibliophile that gave us The Schomburg Center. Charles H. Wesley, Joseph Walkes, Jr. Cornel West, Amos Wilson, and Anthony T. Browder. Malcolm X and Bumpy Johnson were said to have visited the History club and had discussions that lasted until the wee hours of the morning. I dream about just being a fly on the wall. Men such as those who comprised the membership of The Brotherhood of Sleeping Car Porters, many of whom a step away from slavery themselves could not read but saw the importance of collecting books, magazines, and periodicals left behind by passengers to build libraries for their children thus inspiring in them a lifelong vest for reading and learning. Men like John Bruce Grit, Marcus Garvey, Prince Hall, and too many more to name. Malcolm X also famously stated that "Of all subjects to study, history is best suited to reward our research." This statement has had a profound effect on my life and my thinking.

I also have the opportunity to share some stories of inspirational Black people that I wish to bring to the attention of my people who may otherwise not know of them. I also get the opportunity to pay the ancestors back for sending me teachers that gave me insights and information in a world I probably would not otherwise have had. I would not be worth my salt as a so-called historian/sociologist without producing my own scholarly work in book form. I have written hundreds of essays and articles, and a great deal of them have been published. But I cannot shake that feeling of failure I get when my hour is up, and I realize I've only scratched the surface. Without a book written by me in my lifetime, in my sight, life would have been lived in vain.

This book is designed to be an easy read. It is dedicated to the occasional reader who may find big books intimidating and even a little scary. Each chapter is designed to be read in an hour or less. Focus driven and to the point. All the usual suspects won't be found in the contents of this work. Except for Brother Malcolm in whom I have already quoted and referenced twice in this introduction for clarity. (No one can make it plain like Brother Malcolm could).

Instead, I have selected heroes of our great past that may not ring a bell to most. Stories and ideas that hence may have been unfamiliar to the average reader. But to bring these subjects to your attention means I have done my job. I have a love for the written word, eloquence, and the sharpness of well-placed wit and rhetoric. I love when the writer, speaker, or lecturer can, with skill and nuance, make the literal and realistic fade into partnership unnoticed. For instance, a rock is real; you can see it, feel it, pick it up and hold it or throw it. There is no doubt about the realness or realistic nature of the rock. But so too is oxygen. Just as real even though you cannot see it or touch it. So too, is a great idea like that of Black Power. Once explained that to be pro-Black does not mean that you are anti anyone else. Just as the flight attendant on a plane tells you in the event that the cabin becomes depressurized, apply the oxygen mask on yourself first before attempting to help others because you won't be any good to anyone else dead. In this context, Black Power becomes as real as that rock you can see and touch.

In the words of the great John Henrik Clarke, "The African has no friends" we must love us enough to educate and protect us in a world that clearly has no love or mercy for Africa and people of African descent. The inspirational Steven Biko famously titled his book "I write what I like." What a beautiful concept. The Honorable Elijah Muhammad stated in his down home Sandersville, GA manner of speaking, "Don't pay attention to how I'm saying it, just pay attention to what I'm saying." Just as beautiful. My life has been blessed with a myriad of experiences that I would not trade for anything. Experiences that I am convinced would not have been possible without my upbringing in a very southern Jackson, MS birthplace and parents that encouraged every intellectual and extracurricular endeavor. This is a blessing from the universe and one that, unfortunately, all don't get to experience. But it puts a duty on my shoulders, if not a self-appointed duty, to serve Black folk in the diaspora. Hopefully, the introduction of nontraditional people, organizational theories, social structures, and stories of inspiration not commonly known will be my humble contribution to someone's home library and tool of service and inspiration to produce far better works of Black literature for future generations.

So, with this volume, I get to check off two life goals. I get to inform, educate, provide inspiration, motivation, and even entertain all while getting the monkey off my back that I should have gotten rid of decades ago, which is to produce a book worthy of my teachers. To all that read this, I say in the tradition of the African Griot warrior poet/scholars that have gone this way before me in more ways than one. Those that have fought the good fight for Black liberation and paid the price as a result. Those who have risked life and limb to see black people vindicated in every possible field of endeavor and every intellectual and educational pursuit. To all who had risked their lives just to vote or fought in a war for a country that forced you to ride at the back of the bus when European prisoners of war were given more respect. To all of these brave soldiers/veterans of the fight for Black/African liberation, this volume is respectfully dedicated.

CHAPTER 2

OUR LAST GREAT WALK IN THE SUN

(AN INTRODUCTION TO A BLACK COLLEGE FOOTBALL CULTURAL FRAMEWORK)

> *"You are growing into consciousness, and my wish for you is that you feel no need to constrict yourself to make other people comfortable.*
>
> — Ta-Nehisi Coates
>
> Between the World and Me

To some, the meshing together of African American history and Black College football may seem weird. To me, there is no difference. All things concerning African Americans and what they have done, accomplished, invented, and had a prominent role in, is in fact, a part of a much broader narrative that can be told by switching lanes interchangeably. The Southwestern Athletic Conference, better known as the SWAC, has been an indelible fixture in the lives of so many African Americans in the North, South, East, and West in the United States of America and especially mine. I find it hard to tell a story about Mississippi, coming of age in it, remembering my youth and a time in Mississippi way before me, without telling the story and meshing the two.

On June 19th, 1865, the last Africans and persons of African Descent enslaved in the United States of America were freed approximately 2 years after President Lincoln's official Emancipation Proclamation was given on January 1st, 1863. This historic event took place on the Alta Vista Plantation in what is called or referred to now as Walker, Texas. Much of this land which once was a place of misery, hopelessness, and despair for so many Africans and persons of African descent, is now a place of education and advancement for so many Africans and persons of African descent. What the Alta Vista Plantation land now has sitting atop its foundations both figuratively and literally is a Historically Black University serving as a torchlight and hope of a new day coming. The University that I refer to is Prairie View A&M University. Prairie View A&M University is the only original remaining SWAC Member Institution that has been there from beginning to present. In the Akan Twi and many Fante and Mfantsefo languages of the West African Country of Ghana, there is a word called Sankofa. Sankofa is mostly represented by the symbol of a bird with its head turned backward. Sankofa, the word or principle, translates into "retrieve," "fetch," or literally "go back and get it." With that context as a backdrop, let us forever remember our past so that we will never forget our peoples' glorious past and all of its details, the good, the bad, and the truth. If we forget, future generations will never know. I hope from this point forward, my combinations of various subjects intertwined into this narrative not only makes sense to the reader but are also of value.

Dr. John Henrik Clarke and Dr. Yosuf Ben Jochannan, two giant, pioneering figures in the study of the African diaspora would often have friendly yet heated debates over what was ancient Kemit's greatest dynasty? There was plenty to choose from, and incredible arguments on each side. This was the birthplace of science, medicine, mathematics, architecture, the written word, the birthplace of civilization itself. What was not disputed between these two towering intellectuals was the fact that Kemit was our last great walk in the sun. That is before Kemit, and the whole of the African continent was so rudely interrupted by invaders that meant her no good at all. But yet Africans both on the continent and throughout the diaspora are still here. Bloodied but unbowed. As a child coming of age in the state of Mississippi, I was a witness to another of our last great walks in the sun. I saw them all. Jerry "World" Rice, Willie "The Satellite" Totten, Vincent "The Undertaker" Brown, Steve "Air II" McNair, his brother Fred "Air" McNair, Jimmy Smith, and the ferocious "Dark Side" defense. I personally witnessed the great Eddie Robinson, "The Jazzman" W.C. Gordon, "The Godfather" Marino Casem, Archie "The Gunslinger" Cooley, and the colorful "Big" John Merritt wage intellectual warfare of the most epic proportions with one another as translated through some of the biggest, baddest, fastest and powerful athletes ever to don a football uniform. A brief history lesson is in order, even required for younger readers and those unfamiliar with the subject matter of Black College Football.

A certain level of prerequisite information is necessary to make sense of it all. Biddle College, now Johnson C. Smith and Livingstone College, played the first-ever Black College Football game on December 27, 1892. Biddle College now Johnson C. Smith would defeat Livingstone College, and seeing as it was the only game played by any Black Colleges that year, I guess it would be safe to also say that Biddle College now Johnson C. Smith was also the unofficial first-ever Black College National

Champion. Black colleges and universities, for the most part, had been established post-civil war with three exceptions. Cheyney founded in 1837, Lincoln University founded in 1854, and Wilberforce founded in 1856 (the former two in Philadelphia and latter in Ohio) for the sole purpose of educating the newly freed slaves and their children. Another reason was to keep Blacks from attempting to gain enrollment at white institutions of higher education. As far as the gridiron is concerned, this means all of the most talented Black football players had nowhere else to play. No other options were available to them besides Black institutions. For the most part, they could not seek further education anywhere else besides what we would one day call HBCUs.

For example, picture in your mind all of the Black players on Louisiana State University's (LSU) football team transferring to Grambling State University's football team. LSU keeping all of its white players only and the two schools playing a game at a neutral site. Who wins that game? A rhetorical question but a poignant one designed to get you to see the disparity in talent at that time due to segregation. But that was the way it was. White teams from the North and white teams from out West not as hampered with Jim Crow law oftentimes were brave enough to play an HBCU team from time to time but were bested every time. Take for example, two cases, Grambling State's monumental football game played in Tokyo, Japan, in the Tokyo Dome December 11, 1977, resulting in a Grambling victory over Temple by a score of 35-32. Then in 1985, the Oregon State University Beavers traveled down south to Shreveport, Louisiana, to be defeated by Grambling State by the score of 23-6. And on November 19, 1969, the Florida A&M Rattlers defeated the University of Tampa the first time a black university was pitted against a white university in the state of Florida, defeating them by a score of 34-28. On October 6, 1979, at Doak Campbell Stadium, Tallahassee, Florida, A&M defeated the much-vaunted Miami Hurricanes 16-13. Then on October 17, 1981, the Tigers of Tennessee State University (TSU), under the leadership of former Jackson State University (JSU) head football coach "Big" John Merritt, defeated the University of Louisville Cardinals 42-30. Also, on November 10, 1984, under the leadership of one of Merritt's former assistants, now Tennessee State head football coach Bill Thomas, the Tigers once again defeated the University of Louisville Cardinals 24-15.

During the 1968 NFL draft, Jackson State had an astonishing eleven players drafted that year which included offensive tackle Tom Funchess, defensive back Sidney Ellis, defensive end Doug Chatman, defensive back Johnny Outlaw, defensive back Jimmy Holifield, wide receiver, and future Jackson State head football coach Harold "Double O Soul" Jackson, offensive tackle James Jackson, running back Edgar Whipps, defensive back Cephus Jackson, running back Willie Turner and tight end Jimmie Smith. A record certainly never to be broken by any other of Mississippi's collegiate football teams.

The competition was so tough that a future all pro running back with the Philadelphia Eagles named Wilbert Montgomery came to JSU and took one look around at the running back room comprising Eddie Payton, Walter Payton, Rod Phillips, Joe Lowery, and Rickey Young, all of who went on to have playing careers in the NFL. He turned right around and enrolled at Abilene Christian, which ended up being a smart life decision. During Eddie

Payton's senior campaign, the two starting ball carriers were Eddie Payton and a back named Ealey. During the last week of the season, the Tigers had a much lesser opponent coming up on the schedule, and Ealey decided that he would not practice at all that week. The explosive and energy-charged Coach Bob Hill decided to start a freshman in his place. That freshman was Eddie's younger brother, Walter Payton. A bad life decision for Ealey in the midst of so much competition. Mississippi was historically so racist that even once integration was ordered by law in the end, the 'Sip just kept on fighting that good 'ole fight to keep Jim Crow alive.

Ironically, a fact that allowed Jackson State University, Alcorn State University, and Mississippi Valley State University to stay stronger athletically a little longer than many of their sister institutions, well into the decades of the 1980s and 1990s. My father before me, a native Jacksonian, had witnessed in person Walter "Sweetness" Payton, Jackie Slater, Robert Brazil, and the voice you hear during the intro to Marvin Gaye's "What's Going On" the great Lem Barney. All four of these men played at Jackson State University, and all four of them are enshrined in pro football's Hall of Fame. I came onto the scene at the tail end of it all, however, just in time to witness our last great walk in the sun. These histories must be told lest they be forgotten. History should be factual only. Not history by resume. We all leave off those things from our resumes that are not so good or that we would wish to forget or avoid having others to know. But the bad is as integral, sometimes even more so than the pleasant, when it comes to understanding one's history. And eliminating these stories and these histories is an attempt by this country to clean up its resume. To erase her greatest and original sin.

Slavery. There are children on this planet who now ask the question, "Why do black colleges exist?" The answer is simple, slavery. Black colleges and universities exist because slavery existed, and any effort to erase that fact so that future generations would be ignorant of it cannot stand on my watch

CHAPTER 3

THE GOAT, THE EDUCATOR, AND THE JAZZMAN BRING SOUL TO THE VET

"Victory makes your coffee sweeter and your food tastes so much better. It makes your jazz sound smoother, the sun shines brighter. It makes your wife look more beautiful. It even makes you sleep better and dream sweeter. Victory makes all the difference in the world."

- Coach W.C. Gorden

In 1967 for the first time in the storied history of Mississippi Veterans Memorial Stadium (the Vet) in Jackson, MS, two Black College football teams played in a landmark moment in the state's controversial and racist history. The Tigers of Jackson State University swapped paint and traded leather with the great Eddie Robinson's Tigers of Grambling State University. I am sure this would happen to the chagrin and disappointment of the notoriously racist Mississippi governor Ross Barnett. The Vet would become the Blue Bengal's (the Tigers) new home over the coming years. And what perfect opponents for this most monumental of firsts in the state's history. The G-men of Grambling State, as they were affectionately called, was led by an institution of a man. A man who would roam the sidelines, captaining the ship for the

Grambling Tigers for over 57 years. He would go on to become the winningest football coach in college football history, tallying 408 victories prior to his retirement. He produced countless NFL players, future coaches, doctors, lawyers, pastors, and leaders of men. Former players of his brought their sons to play for him. And those sons brought their grandsons. Robinson bragged that he had only one job, one wife, and one mission his entire adult life period.

In a whole lot of ways, the younger coach W.C. Gorden, then an assistant for the JSU football team, felt that the only reason he could make a living doing what he was doing was solely because of Coach Eddie Robinson— leading the G-men for a gob smacking 57 years. This is a feat I can say with ultimate confidence that we will never see duplicated. A dictatorial reign like his in college football will never happen again. Coach W.C. Gorden, who was my favorite football coach of all time, was nicknamed "The Jazzman." It is said that he owned a jazz record collection numbering well over five thousand records. Coach Gorden found similarities between a jazz performance and the game of football. Nothing was more important than the fundamentals to him. Once mastering the fundamentals of the game, such as blocking technique, proper tackling form, and securing the ball with three points of pressure.

Gorden then taught his players that knowing their assignments was vital, also knowing where to be and when to be there. This allowed Gorden's players to get to their assignments fast. At this point, there was room for improvisation. Improvisation is also a key characteristic of any good jazz performer worth their salt. Like the great Miles Davis, who was classically trained at the legendary

Juilliard School of Music in New York City, mastered all the fundamentals of playing his trumpet. But what separated him from his contemporaries was his ability to stay true to the fundamentals whilst improvising a sound never heard before. This is the mark of a great musician. This was also the mark of a great football coach. W.C. Gorden, once head man, was the absolute leader without question. He stated that W.C. stood for "Will cut & Will call yo' momma to come get you." Coach Gorden was the undisputed man. Erudite, resolute, stately, and mean as hell.

At a time when the Ku Klux Klan attacked, brutalized, and murdered black people with impunity in the state of Mississippi, it is important to analyze the backdrop of this monumental game in both a historical and social context. In 1964, three civil rights workers had gone missing. Mickey Schwerner (white) was twenty-four years of age and a recent graduate of Cornell University. Hailing from New York, he traveled to Mississippi to help with Freedom Summer. James Chaney was twenty-one years of age and born and raised a Mississippian. He had been a CORE (Congress of Racial Equality) volunteer since its inception in the state. Chaney was also the only black man in this group of three. Thirdly Andrew Goodman (white) was twenty years of age and a student volunteer who completed the trio. After a night of community work, it came to the attention of fellow activists that three of them had gone missing. In vain, a search began to locate them. All that were involved in the search feared the worst. This was Mississippi, and along racial lines, it was murderous and unforgiving.

This was June 21, 1964. The scene, Neshoba County in a small town called Philadelphia in the east-central part of the state where the three young men were investigating a horrible fire that destroyed a local black church, the handiwork of the Klan. It was also beginning to be suspected that the missing trio was the handiwork of the Klan as well. On August 4, 1964, about six weeks after the trio disappeared, they were found, as many native Mississippians had suspected all along, dead and buried in the rubble of an old dam that had been covered with dirt. It would take another three full years before the seven men guilty of their murders were brought to justice. Also, another first in Mississippi, never in the state's history had any white man been found guilty of killing a black man. Nor had a white person ever been convicted of killing other white people who were sympathetic in aiding in the efforts for civil rights.

It was now 1967, and like Jackson, Mississippi newspapers, both black and white publications, were beginning to announce this historic game about to be played between two Black College football teams for the first time in Mississippi's pride and joy, Mississippi Veterans Memorial Stadium. Built to accommodate overflow and homecoming games for Ole Miss, Mississippi State University, and the University of Southern Mississippi, it had been unquestionably before this game as lily-white as cotton balls in a snowstorm. The same publications, both black and white, were also beginning to make another announcement. Seven men were found guilty in the three murders of Chaney, Goodman, and Schwerner.

Jackson State's head coach Rod Paige and future White House Director of Education were filled with emotions recognizing the ultimate price paid by these young men and civil rights workers. The fact that seven white men, for the first time, had just been found guilty of having killed civil rights workers was almost unbelievable and too much to bear. But there still was a game to be played. Gorden was hired by Page at the beginning of the season, and no one could have imagined that he would become the creator of the famous red and white JSU block and the introducer of red accents into the Tiger's uniforms, which had been for previous decades strictly blue and white with no straying away from official school colors (navy blue and white). This would be Gorden's first time not only coaching against but seeing the legendary Coach Eddie Robinson up close. According to the brilliant book EDDIE ROBINSON "he was the Martin Luther King of football" by Denny Dressman, Coach Gorden, would remember years later that he came out sharp as a tack, a beautiful tie, and carrying a briefcase. I have heard Coach Gorden say that Coach Robinson had an aura that could be felt clear across the field. Gorden stated that he had never seen that level of sophistication in a football coach before then.

In chapter three, on page 158 of Denny Dressman's biography of Eddie Robinson, he quotes Coach Gorden and writes in such a revealing way that allows you to really understand the man and the times he was operating in. He had tried to register to vote in 1960 but failed the test on the U.S. Constitution - even though he taught history and what was then called civics, a class about American government. "The county tax collector administered the test," he said. "It was a subjective test, not an objective test. He'd give you a passage from the Constitution to read, and then you'd give your interpretation of it. Of course, the interpretation you gave was incorrect." Gorden tried again in 1961 and passed, but his wife Vivian, also a teacher, flunked. "It took a lot of courage," Gorden said. "She could have lost her job for trying to register. Mississippians have a love for football, and I think the football coach was treated a little more congenially than the average African American citizen. She's a brave girl. There was no hesitation." Both finally passed - and voted - in 1962.[1]

The Jazzman would get the head coaching job at Jackson State in 1976 and would eventually become the first coach to defeat the legendary Coach Eddie Robinson and his G-men four years in a row. On that day in 1967, the G-men entered the contest undefeated with a 4 and 0 record. Coming off a beatdown of Mississippi Valley State, ending with the tigers defeating the Delta Devils by a score of 68-0. The Blue Bengals were 3 and 1 going into the contest and coming off a close and brutal defensive battle with Southern University, ending in a JSU victory by a score of 3-0. What a battle of quarterbacks. Grambling's legendary James "Shack" Harris versus Jackson State's legendary Robert Kelly. And the QB battle was as advertised. Fourteen to thirteen Gramling going up into the half, fans were set for fireworks coming out. The game ended in a 20-14 victory for the Blue Bengals, capping an emotional day for so many reasons.

The first time two all-black schools were allowed to play in the Vet on the hills of the first-ever conviction of white men for the murder of a Black man and white civil rights workers. These two schools raised the level of football possibilities with talent the Vet's playing surface had never experienced. JSU head coach Rod Paige and his

---

[1] Dressman, Denny. "Eddie Robinson...he was the Martin Luther King of football" (2010). Denver: Comserv Books.

assistant Coach Gorden had also defeated Coach Robinson. What a day. The talent on the field was astronomical, but so was the brilliance of their respective brain trusts. Coach Robinson would go on to become the winningest coach in college football history, not only passing but then blowing by the great Bear Bryant. Coach Gorden would go on to become the winningest coach in JSU football history. And Coach Rod Paige, once done with his coaching career, would go on to serve as the 7th United States Secretary of Education from 2001 until 2005. Paige was appointed by President George W. Bush. This appointment by President Bush made Coach Rod Paige the first African American to serve as the U.S. Chief of Education. Coach Gorden would go on to make the Vet the home of the Tigers and the site of SWAC championships in 1980, 1981, 1982, 1985 (tied), 1986, 1987, 1988, 1990. One black college national championship in 1985 and 28 straight SWAC victories without a loss.

I saw that streak of 28 straight SWAC victories without a defeat come to an end in 1989 against Southern University on a homecoming night under the lights at the Vet as a thirteen-year-old. Later that year, I would witness the defeat of "Iron" Mike Tyson at the hands of James "Buster" Douglass, and both experiences to me felt about the same. Heartbreaking. The Vet was and remained my favorite venue for a collegiate tackle football game, especially under the lights.

CHAPTER 4

THE GODFATHER, THE GUNSLINGER, AND ONE MAGICAL SUNDAY AFTERNOON

"On the East Coast, football is a cultural experience. In the Midwest, it's a form of cannibalism. On the West Coast, it's a tourist attraction. And in the South, football is a religion, and Saturday is the holy day."
- Marino Casem

Sunday, November 4th, 1984, is a day that I will never forget as long as I live. I was witness to the biggest football game ever played in the state of Mississippi. This game was a clash of juggernauts. A matchup of undefeated powerhouses, each having captured the attention of the nation. This game not only enthralled the state of Mississippi but, for a brief moment in history, captured the attention of the collegiate football world. The state's two SEC head coaches were present on the sidelines, having to witness it in person for themselves. First of all, this game was not held on a Saturday but rather on a Sunday. It was televised in the state and surrounding areas and matched against the slate of NFL games scheduled for Sunday viewing. The collegiate game featuring two Black Universities was the hands-down winner, as proven by its record 70 rating share that day.

Jackson State University then head coach W.C. Gorden was guest color commentator alongside Mississippi sportscasting and sports reporting legend Michael Rubenstein and field reporter Clay Hall to round out the broadcast crew for this televised event. This game was originally scheduled for a Saturday in Mississippi Valley's tiny stadium in Itta Bena, MS. The game itself was scheduled long before the 1984 season, as is usually the custom of athletic directors nationwide, but no one could have known at the time of its scheduling that it would ever get this huge. By the time this game was about three weeks away, it was apparent that it had grown way too big for Valley State's stadium and the masses of humanity from near and far that were about to besiege the tiny delta town of Itta Bena. Legendary Mississippi newspaper columnist Rick Cleveland penned tons of articles that I have fond memories, reading. Although a white native Mississippian, Rick was always fair in his writings about the state's three Black schools, and sometimes it seems he gave them more copy. Rick wrote a column in the Jackson Daily News proposing that the game be moved to Jackson's Mississippi Veteran Memorial Stadium. A great idea. The problem was that there were already two ball games scheduled for that Saturday.

One being played on Saturday afternoon, and the other was slotted for that Saturday night. So, the ingenious Rick Cleveland proposed something so crazy it just might work. Cleveland proposed that since the stadium was all booked up on Saturday that the Alcorn State vs. Mississippi Valley game be played on Sunday afternoon. What?!? In the Bible belt?!? A football game played on the Lord's Day?!? In the state of Mississippi?!? Well, in the 'Sip church, folk are football fans too, and churches across the state with permission from their pastors, and in some cases on their pastor's insistence loaded up church buses and choir vans and headed for the Vet. White Mississippians by the thousands came to see the greatest game in the State's history alongside Black fans. The SWAC was the hottest ticket in town, not the SEC.

The isles of Mississippi Veterans Memorial Stadium were occupied with fans, and the steps inside the stadium served as makeshift seats as if designed for that purpose. A special section of seating was rolled out in the open part of the Vets horseshoe and was quickly gobbled up by fans as quickly as it was installed. Officially 62,000 plus, but most believe closer to 65,000 plus packed the Vet netting both HBCUs the biggest paydays in their respective school histories. Mississippi Valley State was undefeated with a 7 and 0 record. Displaying a high-powered, high-flying, aerial assault never seen before. This was the era of the wishbone, the triple option and Power-I, three yards and a cloud of dust. Mississippi Valley State put the ball in the air almost every down. Valley defeated Kentucky State University 86-0 for the first game of their season. Secondly, they massacred the Ichabods of Washburn University 77-15. Then if that was not enough, they defeated the Tigers of Jackson State 49-32 after a twenty-six-year losing streak to the Tigers of Jackson State. This was the game that made people pay attention to tiny Mississippi Valley for the first time in a long time. This was also a game I witnessed, and that night I might add, I witnessed one hell of a mascot fight between the Tiger and the Delta Devil that left the Tiger headless and the Devil bloody. A mascot fight in which people who were there still talk about to this day with differing opinions about who won it.

The Delta Devil's went on to defeat the Southern Jaguars 63-45, then the legendary G-Men of Grambling State 48-36. Now the nation knew this was not a fluke. A few more wins and then a 71-6 curb-stomping of the Prairie View Panthers and now tiny Mississippi Valley State University was ranked #1 in the Black College football poll and ranked #4 in the national NCAA Division I-AA poll. The Alcorn State Braves had been doing just as much butt-kicking if not more themselves, displaying a defense that reduced opponents to very few if any points. Earning a National Black College ranking of 2 and a national NCAA Division I-AA ranking of 3. The only two things more intriguing than these two teams were their two head coaches.

Alcorn State University was led by a man simply known as the Godfather. The great Eddie Robinson withstanding the Godfather, was second only to him in SWAC longevity, leading the Braves of Alcorn since 1966. And Alcorn State had a celebrated football past. Medgar Evers and his older brother Charles Evers had played football for the Braves in the 1950s. Medgar Evers would go down as Mississippi's most iconic figure of the Civil Rights era. Medgar's older brother Charles Evers would become the first Black man elected as mayor of a Mississippi town post-reconstruction, as mayor of Fayette County, Mississippi. The man called simply "The GodFather" Marino Casem was a real firebrand and tough guy. Coach Casem once got into a fight smack dab on the 50-yard line with legendary Jackson State coach Robert "Bob" Hill. This pregame fight is still talked about by those old enough to have witnessed it. A football coach that I had in junior high school told me that the fight started with a slap, but he was looking at a girl in the other direction and did not see who smacked who first, but lord have mercy, the sound of that smack is something he says he will never forget. The fight ended with Marino Casem shirtless and Coach Robert Hill being drug away by authorities and football fans going crazy. Leaving a Roman Colosseum in the gladiator times seems like a prayer meeting. In the stadium, that day, a young man named Walter Payton was a high school senior being recruited by both schools. This was the day he decided to attend Jackson State. Not because his older brother, who was already a star tailback for Jackson State was there, it was because, in his opinion, Bob Hill had won the fight. I have since learned that Coach Bob Hill, notorious for his temper, was the one that smacked Coach Casem first, and then it was on.

Besides being a huge hulking figure that intimidated opponents by his mere presence, Coach Casem produced champions, high pedigree ball teams, and NFL talent, a great orator and a man who was often seen having lunch with the great Muhammed Ali who had started to visit Alcorn State University in an effort to assist predominantly Black Colleges. Coach Casem had produced such men as Leslie Frazier, former shut-down cornerback for the Super Bowl champion 1985 Chicago Bears and head coach of the Minnesota Vikings. The Godfather was the man, and old-school helmet cracking defenses were his forte. If he could not stop Mississippi Valley State's offense, no one could.

On the other side of the coin was a man named Archie "Gunslinger" Cooley. A former fullback and center for the Jackson State Tigers under head coach "Big" John Merritt. The Gunslinger was hired by Coach Merritt once he left Jackson State for the head coaching job at Tennessee State University. Cooley was hired as a linebacker coach.

One of Cooley's responsibilities in this new capacity was to mimic the Tennessee State Tigers' upcoming opponent that week. Cooley studied the previous opponent instead of the next week's opponent and tweaked all the plays that Tennessee State's defense had the most problem stopping. Cooley was playing with alignments and broke with tradition and all conventional wisdom on what an offensive play should look like from center snap to referee's whistle. Soon the Tennessee State defensive at practice could not stop anything Cooley's scout team offenses offered up. Soon the natural roles were reversed, and Cooley's scout team offense was beating up and bullying Merritt's and Coach Joe Gilliam's celebrated defenses. Soon Cooley was named the offensive coordinator by Merritt, and by now, he had an offensive playbook full of the craziest shit anyone had ever seen offensively. Cooley lit up opposing defenses on a weekly basis and soon was offered the head coaching job at Mississippi Valley State in 1980. From 1980 to 1984, Cooley built an offense like none that had ever been seen before. Fielding one of the first, if not the first, all three hundred plus pounds offensive lines. He called them "The Tons of Fun."

Cooley recruited the son of a bricklayer who would become the greatest wide receiver in the history of the sport, the great Jerry "World" Rice. A man who Michael Irving, also a pro football Hall of Famer, called "Jesus Christ with cleats on." For his quarterback, he selected a high school punter who led the state in punting average. His name was Willie "The Satellite" Totten. On one of his recruiting visits to Totten's home, Cooley noticed Totten's abnormally large hands. Cooley said, "Son, I know you can punt, but can you throw?" Cooley thought to himself with hands that big he must have been able to throw. Cooley took Totten to an open field, asked him to throw the football, not to him but just throw it as far as he could. Cooley says he never saw the ball land. That ball disappeared into the sky just like a "satellite," and he had "the world" he was going to have Totten orbit his satellite around. Cooley would line up four wide receivers in a single file line on one side and one receiver on the other, never seeing this before defenses were confused. Do you cover the four and neglect the one? Or do you cover the one and be outmanned on the other side? Whatever you chose to do, you were screwed. On the side with four receivers were sprinters with world-class speed, and on the other side was the slow guy, but he was Jerry Rice, and as we all know, you had to double team Jerry Rice. The spread, run-and-shoot, west coast offense, fun-and-gun, air raid, etc., are all variations of Cooley's offense which he called "the satellite express offense." Oftentimes not huddling and sending in his plays ahead of time, three plays at a time so they could attack at a blistering pace.

Cooley's running back was Carl Bynum, who would later become NFL Hall of Famer Thurman Thomas' lead fullback for the Buffalo Bills. Cooley's defense sported several NFL linebackers, namely Vincent "The Undertaker" Brown. Cooley's coaching staff was full of future head coaches, and Cooley, who was notorious for giving out nicknames, nicknamed them "Cooley and the Gang." The Delta Devils had the swag, and they loved to let it hang out. I remember getting up early that Sunday morning, November 4, 1984, at the age of eight. My father loaded the car up with myself, my mother, and my sister.

We always got to games early. My father and I loved to watch the teams warm up and go through their respective warm-up paces and stretching routines. Also, we got there early to see the bands introduce themselves by marching into the stadium. If you have not seen Jackson State University's "The Sonic Boom of the South" march into the Vet on a Saturday night glaring "Get Ready" by The Temptations in person, then you have not seen a band entrance at all. No one can come up in a house like "Da Boom." On this Sunday, we got there extremely early because my father wanted to avoid the traffic and to ensure our seats were accounted for, and for a good reason. The Vet would soon be a madhouse. Getting there extremely early, we would learn that "The Gunslinger" could make one hell of an entrance himself. While waiting for the first team to hit the field for warmups, a football came flying out of the sky like it had been dropped from an airplane. For close to thirty years afterward, I wondered where in the hell did that football come from? With my attention fixed on that football spiraling from the sky, I, like many others, had not noticed the Valley State receiver that was streaking down the field. He ran a perfect post pattern and neatly ran under that ball, caught it on about the thirty-yard line, and took it the distance to the end zone, and those privileged few already inside the stadium roared with applause.

An eight-year-old at the time, I was losing my mind, and at that very moment, the Mississippi Valley State Delta Devil football team entered the stadium for pregame warmups. What an entrance, the stuff of legends and a moment that I will never forget. I get chills just thinking about all of these years later. Years later, I learned that Cooley would load up a bus of his eleven offensive starters, drive to Jackson from Itta Bena to the Vet every night that week to practice this entrance. He had his offensive starting unit exit the bus, line up in a typical play from scrimmage with a receiver (not Jerry Rice), run around the stadium and enter through one of the open tunnel entrances onto the field and run a post and at a certain point yell and Cooley would signal to Totten to throw the ball. With Cooley's instructions to keep running until you hit pay dirt once he caught the ball. Meanwhile, Totten is under center barking signals while Cooley looked at his watch, timing how long it took his receiver to reach what he knew was the extent of Totten's arm strength. Once he knew his receiver was approaching that distance, Cooley shouted, "Slang it, son," and standing outside of the stadium, Totten threw the ball over the scoreboard in the open end of the Vet as far as he could, reaching Cooley's receiver at about the thirty-yard line. The speedy receiver ran under it, caught it, and the rest was history, as they say. Ingenious!!

I finally found out where that ball came from almost thirty years later. That missing piece of what was maybe the greatest football team entrance I had ever witnessed was well worth the thirty-year wait. The game itself did not disappoint. A pure classic ending in a 42-28 victory for "The Godfather" and his Alcorn State Braves. Mississippi Valley State would rebound from that loss with victories over Alabama State University 49-7 and a slaughter of Langston University 83-11. Memories of this Sunday afternoon with a 2 p.m. kickoff start time had begun about 9 a.m. that morning. Due to traffic produced by the sheer mass of humanity, coming out of the game had us pulling back into the driveway under the darkness of night around 10 p.m. The Godfather and the Gunslinger are legends of a Mississippi HBCU culture that are among the pantheon of greats, including Coach W.C. Gorden. We can argue about the fourth coach needed to complete that Mount Rushmore of Mississippi black college football coaches. But if it were ever completed and you are wondering which of the four gentlemen is Archie "The Gunslinger" Cooley, he is the one wearing the cowboy hat.

There are fancier, more sophisticated, and refined places in this country for sure. Many of which look their noses up at the 'Sip. They downgrade and make fun of the generally accepted notion of what a black Mississippian is supposed to be. If I had to do it all over again, having my choice of anywhere to grow up in the country, I would not pick anywhere else, no other place, except Jackson, MS.

I have learned for many reasons that we represent the bad Negro. In this social context, the oppressor class classified such individuals as "bad" when they cannot be controlled or intimidated, which means that in the hearts of Blacks, such individuals were loved and admired and inspired other Blacks to behave in the same fashion. Good in the Black cultural expression vernacular is oftentimes expressed with the word bad. Hence a bad car translates into you thinking it's a good car. Of course, in the African American cultural vernacular, bad in this context becomes good. The Bad Negro did not run. The Bad Negro chose to stay and fight. The Bad Negro never left kin behind. The Bad Negro was called "bad" by the oppressor class, then becoming beloved by his own community. So the African American cultural expression dictated a flipping of the words' meaning. This message of pride in oneself was explained in a very sociological manner to me at a very young age by an older Black man who had probably never even heard the term sociological. Being a native Mississippian, he listened to me asking him questions about his recent visit to the North. He answered my questions by saying, "Son, it's Mississippi for me and nowhere else. I love being a Negro from Mississippi, which means I am a Bad Negro. All the scared Negros ran north." In a speech being given in Greenwood, MS, revolutionary and master organizer Stokely Carmichael responded to a reporter's question regarding their level of fear, "All the scared Negros went to Chicago." What that older gentleman said to me stuck with me all of my life. I liked that.

So, I chose to live that. I am that. To make it and survive in such an oppressive environment requires a certain attitude, one that says I won't take no stuff. An attitude is required if you want to maintain your sanity no matter your circumstances and live as a man and not as a boy. This was the lesson being relayed to me, and even as a child, I was paying attention. The mind is a complicated thing, especially to those of us that do not fully understand it and its intricate workings. In the recesses of my mind, whenever I see Alcorn State and Mississippi Valley State play, no matter how good or bad they currently are, I see this day. In a nutshell, what that older gentleman was trying to convey to me was accomplished. We always knew that historically on the gridiron, we were better. On a crisp November Sunday in 1984, everyone else knew it too. Ain't gone let nobody turn me around, and we don't turn no jaws. That is Black Mississippi. What a way to spend a Sunday afternoon.

The state of Mississippi and its heroes of the gridiron from years gone by are still remembered by those who know the truth. Earlier this year (2021), The National Football Foundation (NFF), in conjunction with the College Football Hall of Fame, released its nominees for the 2021 College Football Hall of Fame. There were a total of 99 football players and 33 coaches selected for the divisional entrees. Among those worthy men were 8 football players and 2 coaches from the Historically Black College and University ranks. Among the HBCU nominees were 5 Black College players from the SWAC's Mississippi member institutions.

One of my favorite linebackers to watch growing up was nominated. Mississippi Valley State's Vincent "The Undertaker" Brown. Brown was twice selected as All-SWAC and led the Delta Devils in tackles his sophomore, junior and senior campaigns. Brown also led the nation in tackles in 1986 and 1987. "The Undertaker" set an all-time record with 570 registered career tackles. Brown was selected NCAA All-American in 1987.

Mississippi Valley State's Parnell "Pay Dirt" Dickerson a 1975 Pittsburgh Courier All-American and Pittsburgh Courier National Player of the year his senior campaign was selected. "Paydirt" completed his career at MVSU as the SWAC's all-time leader in total offense with an astounding 7,442 yards compiled. A starter since his freshman year, he set MVSU record for scoring his freshman year with 21 touchdowns. And again, his junior season with 26 touchdowns scored. Parnell was named the State of Mississippi's College Player of the Year in 1975. Parnell finished with a record 89 touchdowns scored. In 1976 "Pay Dirt" was drafted by the Tampa Bay Buccaneers in the 7th round of the NFL Draft. This made Parnell "Pay Dirt" Dickerson the first African American Quarterback the franchise had ever drafted. Parnell kicked down the door for future Super Bowl XXII MVP Grambling State University's Doug Williams.

Alcorn State University's Dennis Thomas was also selected as a nominee. Thomas was a two-time Pittsburgh

Courier first-team All-American in 1972 and 1973. Playing the center position for the Braves of Alcorn, Thomas is the only offensive lineman in SWAC history to be named the SWAC's offensive MVP back in 1973. Thomas was the Bell Cow of the Braves' 1970 SWAC Championship team.

Finally, rounding out the SWAC Mississippi member institution players selected for the 2021 College Football Hall of Fame ballot is Mississippi Valley State's Ashley Ambrose. Cornerback and Punt returner for the Delta Devils, Ambrose led the Nation in punt returns during his senior season. In 1991 Ashley was named both an NCAA All-American and ALL-SWAC First-Team Defensive selection.

CHAPTER 5

THE FEVER

"The gridiron is a laboratory for manhood."

Coach Jake Gaither

Tackle football was the undisputed pastime of 1980's Mississippi. Football was king. Like all boys my age at the time, I had caught the football fever at the age of three. My parents allowed me to try out for my elementary school's football team in the fourth grade. I was nine years old, and I was a fairly big kid bursting at the seams. My school was named Holy Family Catholic School, which was about a five-minute drive from our home on Pine Island Dr., or about a twenty-minute or so walk home after school. Holy Family was an all-Black Catholic school with a black man as the head priest. His name was Father Joe. My family was not Catholic by any means, but this was an excellent school with caring community folks who put the children enrolled in the school first and foremost. All Black because this was Mississippi, after all, a state desperately holding on to a Jim Crow way of life that demanded the separation of blacks and whites socially, especially whenever children were concerned.

I was successful in making the team, and it was a moment of accomplishment in my life as special to me as my graduation from college. The first two positions I was assigned to play were center of offense and middle linebacker on defense. Holy Family only had roughly about

15 or so kids on the team. So, playing iron man football, meaning going both ways, was required in order to have a season. What a privilege this was because unbeknownst to me at the time was the fact that there were three positions in the game of football that would teach you the entire game, unlike none of the others that at that age taught you your position but not necessarily the game. Those three positions were center, middle linebacker, and quarterback. The reason being is, since the person playing any of these three positions not only had to learn and master their own personal duties and the in's and out's that came with that position, but all of your teammates as well on your side of the ball. And I had been assigned two out of those three.

As a center, once I mastered the center snap exchange. I had to learn each of the other offensive line man's responsibilities because the center was responsible for recognizing what blocking scheme was needed to make the play that was called successful. Also, at the center, I was responsible that every one of my offensive teammates reported immediately to the huddle, usually yelling "huddle up" following a play. Also that they received and understood the play, remembered the snap count, and then breaking my teammates from the huddle with a strong, crisp clap of the hands. I had to learn each person's blocking assignments in order to make corrections and call out changes when I recognized a different defensive package or spotted a blitz was coming.

On defense, which has always been my favorite side of the ball, my position was middle linebacker. The middle linebacker position was particularly a manly one. The linebackers were the tough guys. A linebacker was supposed to be big and strong enough to fight off and shed the blocks of offensive linemen, usually the biggest kids on the field. A linebacker also had to be fast enough to cover running backs coming out of the backfield for screen passes and elongated toss sweeps. Most importantly, the middle linebacker had to be smart enough to outthink the opposing quarterbacks. In fact, the middle linebacker is the quarterback of the defense. The middle linebacker made all of the signal calls, interpreting for the rest of the defense what the coach wanted to have carried out on the field.

As a middle linebacker, I had to know not only what I was supposed to be doing but what all of my comrades were supposed to be doing as well. I was the field coach, and the game became for me just as analytical as it was physical. You also as a linebacker, have to be a tough guy. The position comes with a lot of physical contacts. If you do not naturally love the contact, you're not a linebacker. Even if you like the contact but just not all of the time or only with smaller players, that is also not good enough. Linebacker requires you to love the contact, craving it. No shying away from contact with bigger, stronger players and flying into the fray headfirst to address that lead fullback coming at you at full speed without hesitation or concern for your physical welfare.

The whole of Mississippi was on fire for football. Especially college football. As is not the case for so many African American boys growing up where I did, our focus was not on any of the major White teams in the State like it is now for this current generation of kids playing football, but instead, our focus was placed squarely on the states. There is an elite band of Black Colleges playing a brand of football we called SWAC Football. These three were the Jackson State University Tigers, the Alcorn State

University Braves, and the Mississippi Valley State University Delta Devils and the rest of the teams located outside of the state belonging to the Southwestern Athletic Conference or, for short, "The SWAC." This was and is the most storied conference in Black College football without question. Sure, we had three major white schools playing quality football in the State, two of which belonged to the SEC or the Southeastern Conference, a powerful white college sports conference that had the monopoly on televised football in the State of Mississippi.

The two SEC schools were The University of Mississippi and Mississippi State University. The University of Southern Mississippi was independent at the time. But they were an afterthought for us in my neighborhood. The SWAC schools in the State were still very strong and as powerful as the big White institutions, and they were scared to death of putting one of the Black schools from the state on their schedules. It is hard to promote white supremacy when you just got your hat handed to you on a football field by an all-Black team which was dramatically more underfunded than they were.

In what can only be called the laboratory of manhood, the football field was the great equalizer. So old school Jim Crow traditions and customs enforced by White vigilante violence for generations in the State demanded that these schools never mix it up on a gridiron. , This is one of the social phenomena inside the inner workings of Mississippi that allowed the big three Jackson State, Alcorn State, and Mississippi Valley State to stay as strong as they did for as long as they did, well into the 1980s and the 1990s, when our other sister institutions located outside of the state had long ago been weakened by integration and the mad rush of white college football programs efforts to gobble up as much of the Black talent in order to win championships, by having a better level of athlete that the law had prevented them from getting in the Jim Crow past. For the Black ball player now able to attend these white institutions, that helped lure them with facilities and stadiums unlike any that a Black school could stack up against. Combined with the opportunity to play on television was too tempting to pass up.

A couple of years, maybe a decade at the most, and the balance of power had shifted on the field. But in the state of Mississippi, we still felt the unmistakable feeling of disdain coming from the Power White Institutions (PWI) around us. Nothing is a better anti-recruiting tool than a stadium full of White people waving Confederate flags cheering a team whose school mascot was Confederate Civil war Rebel roaming the sidelines waving a Rebel flag himself during Ole Miss Football games. They did not like us; they did not want us there, and they made sure we knew it.

What will always stay etched in my memory was the game day and game night experience we got when Mississippi Veterans Memorial Stadium was double booked. Oftentimes one of the big white schools would play during the day, and Jackson State would be booked to play that night, usually with a 7 pm or a 7:30 pm kick-off. On those occasions, the stadium was filthy, littered with trash, the seats smeared with mustard and ketchup, and sometimes racial taunts and shouts filled with profanity from cars full of whites driving back to Oxford, Starkville, or Hattiesburg following the conclusion of the early game. Clearly, they did not feel that an African American deserved to enjoy a ball game in a place that should have been only theirs by birth right. Coupled with the fact that the game we were about to witness featured more future NFL draft picks than their game.

See, all Mississippi schools at this time were sharing the 62,000 plus Mississippi Veterans Memorial Stadium and using it for homecoming and big rivalry games when the relative to other states' tiny campus stadiums would not accommodate the crowds expected. Today Jackson State University is the owner of The Vet. Once the White schools built big modern stadiums on their respective campuses, the state government planned to tear the old Vet down. But Jackson State still needs it for its huge crowds that lead the nation in attendance for decades on the Division I-AA and FCS levels. Sometimes we had the stadium all to our Black selves while the PWI's played on their respective campuses or out on the road, and the stadium would be immaculate. Nothing could beat or top the experience of a night game at The Vet under the lights. Still, my favorite place to attend a fall football game, and I suspect that is a fact of my life that will never change.

My father took me to my first Football game when I was 3 years of age. The year was 1979, and unbeknownst to me, it was a big rivalry game. Jackson State University vs. Southern University. The Tigers vs. The Jaguars. The Sonic Boom of The South vs. The Human Jukebox. Now called the BOOMBOX Classic, named for the two schools' world-famous powerhouse marching bands. My two favorite Marching Bands in the World. I still remember the smell of cigars and the smoke of more than a few barbeque grills going simultaneously alongside fish frying and the sound of The Blues, Zydeco, and Southern Soul music blasting from radios and stereo systems. I was super young, only 3 years of age, but I was in heaven. I still can remember the final score, which was Jackson State University 34 and Southern University 0. That memory is always a pleasure not only because the Tigers whupped the Jaguars but also because my first ever football game was the real deal.

That SWAC matchup is bedrock tradition, and it gets no better than that. Also, a big-time memory for me is the fact that learning and trying to understand the score as it increased by the quarter is how I learned my numbers and how to count. I will never forget my Father's final math lesson of the night as we exited The Vet. Me saying, "Daddy did we win?" and my dad replied, "Yeah, son, Thirty-four beats Zero, and nothin' from nothin' leaves nothin'."

I had been spoiled, my first HBCU experience was a massive one, and I was hooked. Hooked on it all, the food, the music, the marching bands, even the mascots. But most of all the crazy, yet intriguing game being played on the field that I didn't understand. Six years later, I became a linebacker and center on my school's fourth-grade football team and a carrier of these traditions that I enjoy and hold so dear. My father, who took me to that game at the age of three, is responsible for making me an HBCU man, and that first experience made me a football player. Soon, I would be inspired by a group of four that I credit with giving me a standard to emulate, study and idolize. Enter "The Darkside."

*** My father, Dr. Samuel L. Polk, Sr. designed the Jackson State University Centennial Monument on the Campus of Jackson State University placed on campus in 1977. I never visit the campus without visiting it.

CHAPTER 6

THE DARK SIDE

"The opportunity to secure ourselves against defeat lies in our own hands."

- Sun-Tzu

I love all Historically Black Colleges and Universities. Primarily because they have historically meant so much to so many African Americans in this country, changing the lives of so many newly freed from the bonds and horror of that most peculiar institution and America's original sin. Slavery. Also, HBCU's have meant so much to Africans from the continent as well as for Africans from across the global African diaspora. Make no mistake about it, the Jackson State Tigers have been my favorite football team since the age of three. The Tigers never look as impressive and intimidating as they do when performing the team's famous chant before games during pre-game warm-ups. Those chants were led by an iconic figure of a man named Edward Langford Lipscomb, affectionately known to most as "Lip." He was a role model to many and, for over 40 years, a volunteer Dad, also the honorary coach for the JSU Tigers. In 1987, in a Clarion-Ledger article on him, he stated that he considered the ball club family. The chant he leads the entire team in went something like this:

"WE GOT A TEAM BY GOLLY, WE GOT A TEAM

WE GOT A TEAM BY GOLLY, WE GOT A TEAM

WE GONNA FIGHT BY GOLLY, WE GONNA FIGHT

WE GONNA FIGHT BY GOLLY, WE GONNA FIGHT

WE GONNA WIN BY GOLLY, WE GONNA WIN

WE GONNA WIN BY GOLLY, WE GONNA WIN"

Mr. Lipscomb became an ancestor on May 10, 1997, and his chant is stuck in my mind 'til this day. So many times, trying to figure out what they were actually screaming on the field from so far away. Reminiscent of a scene out of the movie "300", during that chant, it didn't look like playing a tackle football game with that bunch was a healthy idea or certainly not a safe one indeed.

Sometime before the start of the 1985 football season, Coach James Carson, defensive coordinator for the Jackson State University Tigers football team, traveled to the Chicago Bears training facility to study this new "forty-six" (46) devised by a brilliant defensive mind named Buddy Ryan, defensive coordinator for the NFL's Chicago Bears. I have heard rumors that Coach Ryan actually got the defense from Coach Joe Gilliam, a legendary coach who had historical stats at Jackson State University as defensive coordinator under the legendary "Big" John Merritt, and he followed him to Tennessee State University in the same capacity as head of defensive operations, eventually becoming a head coach himself.

Nevertheless, Coach Carson was so impressed that he returned to Jackson State University and installed it. The forty-six defense is not what most people think. It's not like the four-three (4-3) defense which is a four-three base set, four down lineman, and three linebackers. Also, it is different from a three-four (3-4) which is a three-four base set, three down linemen, and four linebackers. The forty-six's name did not reflect the base set. It got its name in a much different way. The forty-six required that at least one defensive player blitzed every snap. Usually, it was a strong safety named Doug Plank. In its developmental stages, Ryan would call for Plank to blitz before each snap. The problem was Coach Ryan was always bad with names, and as usual, he never could remember Doug Plank's name. Plank's jersey number was 46. So, Coach Ryan called out before the snap, "Hey 46, you know what to do." So, it became known as the "46" or the "Bear Forty-Six."

It was extremely complicated and extremely aggressive, often sending three, sometimes as many as four defensive players after the quarterback every play. Coach Carson's tiger defense mastered practicing, sometimes three times a day in an era where that was admired as opposed to frowned upon in today's athletic climate. By the 1987 season, the tiger defense was almost impenetrable. I was by now starting my third season of organized tackle football and still a center on offense and a middle linebacker on defense. Still going to all home games with my father, I naturally watch with much enthusiasm.

But something had happened by then that was much different in terms of how I now watched the game. I no longer watched it like a fan. I was now a full-fledged football player, and football players don't watch plays from scrimmage, instead, they study film live. I was now picking out tendencies, reading offenses, and learning every move and idiosyncrasies of my favorite players. Of course, my favorite players were the linebackers. The 1987 JSU Tiger defense led the nation in almost every category. Negative rush yards or single-digit rush yards allowed was a constant result following games. The defensive line was tremendous with a few future NFL draft picks. The secondary was just as stingy also with a couple of future NFL draft picks. But those linebackers, WOW!!!!

That defense had picked up the moniker "The Darkside-Defense." It was sunshine and the rainbows from the center back. But in front of the center was total darkness. Triple stage darkness. A darkness that opposing ball carriers entered but didn't escape. All being orchestrated by those low down, freaky LB's, those head-splitting, tooth chipping, red Nike shoe wearing, no rush yards allowing, quarterback crushing, nasty linebackers from JSU.

Starting with the first of the four that caught my attention as a ten-year-old. Dennis "D.C." Conner, number 54, 5'11" and 245 pounds, hailing from Tuscaloosa, Alabama, and playing the weak end, which was a linebacker on the weak side that blitzed each and every snap. The second was Andre' "Freak" Lloyd, number 58, hailing from Brookhaven, Mississippi, 6'2" and 248 pounds. Playing the position of weak side linebacker and lining up on the weak side meaning away from the tight end side. Third was Jammie Collins, number 55, hailing from Brookhaven, Mississippi as well. He was 6'1" and 225 pounds. Playing the position of a middle linebacker, a position he started at for four years straight. He was the signal-caller. And last but not least, there was Darion "Big Lazy" Conner (no relation to Dennis). Hailing from Prairie

Point, Mississippi, number 56, 6'3" and 250 pounds, running the 40-yard dash in 4.5 seconds. Playing the position of strong side linebacker.

This aggregation of aggression was scary, they were devastating. Nowadays, they split the pregame field into two halves. Fifty yards a piece for both teams warm-up stretches with a line down the middle that you cannot cross. This is done to avoid pre-game fights. But in 1987, the JSU linebackers, during pregame warmups, circled the entire field. Walking through opposing teams, stretch routines, and warmups trash-talking and intimidating opposing offenses. And after watching their game film all week, they knew what those nasty linebackers were saying was true, and it was about to happen to them.

They were a four-headed monster that comprises my favorite football players collegiately. I cannot pick just one of them as a unit. They are my favorite college players, and I might add the best linebacker package I ever witnessed with my own two eyes. Everything they did, I tried to do. I was often getting into trouble for my efforts. They all wore red Nike sneakers. On that day, football cleats came in two colors primarily, black and white. Ordering shoes late that season, the factory was out of black cleats and white cleats. All they had left were red cleats—unheard of at the time. Coach W.C. Gorden said, perfect, and the rest was history. "Them" red Nike shoe boyz had an unmatched swagger. They wore red socks, and Darion even put a red sock over his neck roll, making it appear red from the factory from my vantage point from the stands. I painted my football cleats and neck roll red using a red magic marker, getting myself into hot water for what was viewed as a lack of responsibility and a lack of respect for my things that had been paid for by others. I did not care, I was on the "Darkside" of things now. During the 1987 season, Jackson State played the University of Southern Mississippi (USM), a white power institution that regularly played the likes of Alabama, Florida State, and the University of Pittsburgh.

It was the first time a black college played a white college in the entire history of the state. A huge underdog, JSU outplayed USM in all phases of the game except one. There are three phases of football. Number one is offense, two is defense, and the third is special teams. The Tigers outperformed the Eagles in the offense. JSU's star running back and all-time rushing leader broke all of JSU's most famous football player's records, the great Walter Payton. His name was Lewis "No Frills" Tillman, and he compiled more rushing yards than the Eagles entire offensive yardage output. At halftime, the Darkside defense held USM to minus offensive yards, and mid-way through the third quarter, the game was scoreless. This historical game was held in the "Rock" USM's home stadium in Hattiesburg, Mississippi. And it was responsible for USM's first home game sell-out in school history. I left out a major point. Guess who USM's starting quarterback was? It was none other than future NFL great Brett Favre. "Freak" Andre Lloyd knocked him out of the game early, the only time Favre was ever knocked out of a college game in his entire collegiate career. Brett Favre has said that it was the hardest he had ever been hit in his entire football career, college or professional. Unfortunately, the Tigers were bested in the last phase of football, special teams. Missed field goals and a punt returned for six were the difference. The Darkside allowed only one offensive touchdown the entire game.

Lewis Tillman rushed for more yards than the entire USM offense and scored a touchdown. But the final score was USM 17, JSU 7. USM head coach Jim Carmody said that JSU's defense was the best defense he had ever seen and that when those linebackers tackle you, you stay tackled. He also said that Jackson State was as good as or better than any team they had faced that season, including the University of Alabama, Mississippi State, and Florida.

Dennis Conner would go on to a legendary coaching career of his own. Spending ten years at HBCU Stillman College in his hometown of Tuscaloosa, AL, as a defensive coordinator and an educator. Dennis spent twenty-plus years at Central High School, where he has sent over thirty students to Jackson State, and all but two graduated earning degrees in a multitude of fields and disciplines. Andre' Lloyd went on to play with the New England Patriots, Los Angeles Rams, New Orleans Saints, and the Hamilton Bear Cats of the Canadian Football League. Once done with football, Andre rose to become chief of police in Yazoo County, Mississippi. Cammie Collins, picked up as a free agent for the Pittsburg Steelers, became a success off the field as well in the over-the-road trucking industry. Darion Conner was drafted in the second round of the 1990 NFL draft by the Atlanta Falcons, also playing with the Charlotte Panthers and New Orleans Saints. Jackson State's defense was always about intimidation.

Coach Carson's Darkside defense always had size, speed, and attitude. They specialized in being nasty. That specialization was not always restricted to downs from scrimmage from whistle to whistle. They were, in fact, bullies. In the late 1980s, the Tigers were in Montgomery,

Alabama, to play SWAC Conference opponents, the Alabama State University Hornets. Ironically, Alabama State was Jackson State's first-ever opponent at the start of the Tiger's football program, playing them back in 1911. Some Alabama State Hornets players during this particular road game for the Tigers that I reference in the late 1980s were stretching during pre-game warm-ups in the endzone. Then the linebackers from JSU took possession of the field and particularly that endzone. Out of nowhere, All-American, All-Swac, and future 2nd round NFL draft pick of the Atlanta Falcons Darion Conner slapped the hell out of an Alabama State Hornet and began a chant with his linebacker brothers, "Whose house? LB's house!" The 6'2" 250 Conner was so intimidating it hardly got a reaction, but mentally the point was made. We are on the road, but we are here, and now the Darkside was in the house. And the house was theirs.

One day, I reached out to Dennis to see if I could interview him for my podcast "The Melanated Power Hour," he agreed, and that episode became very popular. He called me the day after it aired and told me, "You know I could get all four of us on the show if you want. "My mouth fell open, and I jumped, and my head hit the ceiling. That episode was even more popular, and it was the first time since that historic 1987 season that all four of them had been together in conversation in thirty-four years. I am so proud that I was able to help bring them back together after all that time. I am glad to say that they are not just my childhood gridiron heroes, they are now my friends. And four of the nicest men one could ever know. But to me, they will always be those freaky LB's, those tooth-breaking, head-splitting, no rush yard allowing, pick-six scoring, red shoe wearing, low down nasty linebackers from JSU. Darkside Forever!

** I was able to wear all four of my linebacker hero's jersey numbers during my playing career from elementary school right up to college. A fact that I am very proud of.** In the 4th grade, my first jersey # was 54. (Holy Family Elementary School Wildcats)

** In the 6th grade, it was #58. (Holy Family Elementary School Wildcats)

** In the 8th grade, it was #55. (Powell Jr. High School Trojans)

** And finally, in college, it was #56. (Lane College Dragons)

CHAPTER 7

FINE TUNE YOUR SENSORY APPARATUS

> "So, fiddley-dee, fiddley-dum
> Look out, baby, 'cause here I
> come."
> - Temptations

It was 1979 when my father took me to my first Black College Football game at the age of three, I have memories of walking up the ramp after entering the stadium and into a dark tunnel which all of a sudden exploded into lights, sights, sounds and smells that are unforgettable for me. A 7:00 pm kick-off under the lights in the Vet packed with frenzied football fans. I had no idea at the time that this glorious event would become my first love and the doorway for me finding my passion, history. A football player to the core, ironically, the first thing that caught my attention that day was the tiger mascot, whom I loved. The second thing that caught my undivided attention, my eyes, my ears as well as my imagination, were the bands. Partly due to the fact that the respective football teams had not yet appeared.

The game had not started, but already these two bands were locked in battle. It was total warfare. It was Jackson State University's (JSU) Sonic Boom of the South vs. Southern University's (SU) Human Jukebox, two of the loudest, most entertaining ever to do it. It gets no better than this as far as marching band battles go. And I loved it, the louder, the better. That eardrum destroying, ratchet cranking, blowin' non-stop with funk and soul, uniquely produced only by a SWAC marching band. And these two monsters of music did it best. SWAC STYLE!!! I am hooked on this cultural expression of third space theory, and I am not alone. Usually referred to as "band heads," there is a subgroup of brothers and sisters that follow this sport as intensively as the sport of football. Marching sport or marching season. The BOOM vs. THE BOX is always special. Styles make fights, and this is the ALI/FRAZIER of marching prize fighting.

The very next game my father took me to was the "Soul Bowl," the inter-state rivalry between Jackson State and Alcorn State, the Tigers vs. the Braves. What I heard Michael Rubinstein once call on the local Jackson news sports segment, "The annual love in or bloodbath, take your pick." What I remember most about this one was arriving at the stadium even earlier than before. This time, the greatest marching band entrance there is or ever was or ever will be, was about to materialize right before my eyes. JSU's marching band, The Sonic Boom of the South, since the 1960s, has played their version of the Temptations Motown classic "Get Ready" as the school's unofficial fight song. When they march into a stadium with it, the battle is usually over before it starts, i.e., an "IRON" Mike Tyson circa 1987 ring entrance. No one, and I mean no one, can make an entrance like the BOOM.

Being in SWAC country, I was privileged to see them all frequently. They included Southern University's "The Human Jukebox," Alcorn State University's "Sounds of Dyn-O-Mite," Texas Southern University's "The Ocean of Soul," Mississippi Valley State University's "Lean Mean Green Marching Machine," Grambling State University's

"World Famed," Prairie View A&M University's "Marching Storm," Alabama State University's "Marching Hornets" and various other non-SWAC Conference bands like Florida A&M University's (FAMU) "Marching 100." But no one does it like the SWAC. And as I write, FAMU is now a SWAC Conference member institution along with Bethune Cookman University. At a SWAC game, no one goes to the bathroom or the concession stands during halftime.

In fact, for a large segment of those gathered, halftime is the only reason they bought a ticket. Being honest, I must admit that I enjoy the battles of the bands from the stands more than the field shows. The reason being most assuredly can be attributed to my first experience so many years ago walking into that immense battle already raging in the stands between JSU and SU. Today this is called the "Zero Quarter." Immediately following the conclusion of the football game, another and final battle is fought between the two opposing marching bands called the "Fifth Quarter." I never leave a game until the conclusion of the "Fifth Quarter." A tradition I observe in reverence 'til this day.

I enjoy hip-hop, more so as a younger man. However, my favorite musical traditions born in the African Diaspora have always been Blues and Jazz. This is due to two forms of social conditioning. The first is Mississippi is the birthplace of the Blues. I was fully immersed in the cultural expressions of it. The Blues was inescapable. The second reason is the fact that these African music forms use instrumentation, brass horns, and drums. This from an early age has always reminded me of Historically Black Colleges and Universities (HBCU) marching bands and the creativity they manifest. Especially the New Orleans style 2nd Line bands that march during what is called parade season. In the 'SIP, any excuse we can come up with to have a parade will do.

The Sonic Boom of the South has always been my favorite. Soulful, funky, aggressive, and loud as hell. "The Tiger Run On" is a smooth yet static, staccato, staggered, deliberate march, culminating in a wave-like sprint is how the Boom traditionally enters onto the field to start off a halftime performance. I miss "The Voice of The Boom," who passed away a while back, Dr. Jimmie James. He was the official voice and announcer for the Tiger marching band. He was a legend and legendary for his intellectual trash talking. It was never vulgar, instead, it was educated, using a barrage of thousand-dollar words that would make any Harvard professor of English beside themselves with envy. He was James Earl Jones meets Muhammad Ali. Dr. James could bring them out with authority, and while on the mic as the Boom was starting "The Tiger Run On," he sounded something like this:

"NOW, LADIES AND GENTLEMAN! FINE TUNE YOUR SENSORY APPARATUS FOR THE UTMOST, THE ACME AND PINNACLE OF THE MOST EXQUISITE SIGHTS AND SOUNDS FOUND IN ANY BAND PERFORMANCE ANYTIME AND ANYWHERE; FOR THE PRETERNATURAL, THE MOST DELIGHTFUL AND DELECTABLE SIGHTS AND SOUNDS AVAILABLE TO ANY AUDIENCE ANYTIME AND ANYWHERE. FRIENDS, IT'S THE APEX OF EXCELLENCE, THE COMPENDIUM OF PRETENTIOUS, OSTENTATIOUS, POMPOUS, AND PALATIAL VARIETY, THE MOST ASTONISHING,

GARGANTUAN, PRODIGIOUS, STUPENDOUS, SAVORY, AND PALATABLE AGGREGATION, REPRESENTING THE AGE OF THE ELECTRONIC AND COMPUTERIZED MUSICAL EXPLOSION. OBSERVE THE QUICKNESS, THE ECCENTRICITY, AND THE AGGRESSIVE SHOWMANSHIP OF THIS OUTSTANDING AGGREGATION. JACKSON STATE UNIVERSITY PROUDLY PRESENTS THE QUINTESSENCE OF CONTEMPORARY SOUNDS AND MANEUVERS, THE SUMMA CUM LAUDE OF BANDS, THE FAMOUS SONIC BOOM OF THE SOUTH".

And with that oratorical gift, like a Baptist preacher in the African American call and response tradition finely tuned in country churches scattered across the deep South and before that molded in the fire of affliction on plantations in an era of legal slavery, and even before that in West Africa, the land of our ancestors' genetic memory was exercised. Dr. James whipped up the crowd into a frenzy. People would exclaim shouts of "Amen," "tell 'em Doc," "talk man," and "you preachin' now." The stage was now set, and it was on! My Uncle Howard, who always sat next to us, would always say, "That brother said somethin' there" and "Go head mane." And if the Boom was not enough, add in the J-Settes, JSU's majorette squad often imitated even by the likes of Beyonce; Wavee Dave, the incomparable Tiger mascot; and the hardest group of drum majors ever to exist, made it difficult to compare or compete with them, damn near impossible.

In 1975 in Jackson, Mississippi, former JSU Band members Caleb Tyrone Armstrong, Ray Smith, Joe Leslie, David Thigpen, Victor Mason, Larry Addison, Adolph

Adams, and Robert Black formed a Soul Group called "Freedom." In 1979 the group recorded a song for Jackson-based Malaco Records that would blow up big time on a national scale. The single was entitled "Get Up and Dance." It is one of the most sampled songs in hip-hop. It has been sampled by the likes of Grand Master Flash & The Furious Five, KRS-ONE, SWV, and featured on movie soundtracks like "Above the Rim" and "New Jack City." It was also used by comedian Chris Rock as intro music to hype up his crowds on stage and television.

One thing I will always miss is the way the SWAC marching bands would play almost non-stop in the stands. So loud at times, it caused their respective football teams delay of game penalties. Even after protests from each school's respective head coaches to each other to please stop, the band played on. Referee warnings fell on deaf ears. The SWAC was indeed the Wild, Wild West. Man, do I miss the SWAC of my youth, from JSU's "Get Ready" to Alcorn's "Cherokee" and Mississippi Valley's "Devil's Gun," originally performed in 1977 by C.J. & Company, a great R&B/Soul band back in the day. This was the soundtrack of my life. Today, however, due to black institutions of higher learning's problematic financial situations, multi-billion-dollar companies are buying ad space at games and paying big money to have their companies commercials play over the P.A. system, which has caused these great bands to become somewhat silenced.

This is why the Zero Quarter and the Fifth Quarter are so important. Like always, Black people find a way. And these are two of the ways those traditions are being kept alive for future generations. Playing in what is sometimes referred to as "Fortanpo-Fortissimo," or as a well-known Black College band director explained to me, means "Loud as mutha fuckin' possible." Back in the day, too much was at stake to stop blowin'. Just as war was being fought on the gridiron, another war was being fought in the stands, and it was a war being fought for the minds and hearts of young future college students and recruits for their institutions. A war I always got even as a football player. To take an "L" in front of crowds that size could potentially dim the light of your school and its attractiveness to potential students. So many students choose their school and even chose an HBCU instead of a PWI (white power institution) because of the band, and a single performance that they may have seen at a classic or homecoming game and such an impression was left on them that their mind was made up from that day forth where they would attend after high school. I can't hear a classic marching band song on the radio like Cameo's "Neck," "Knight by Knight," or "Skin I'm In" without pointing out to the uninitiated that that's where it came from. Jackson State's version of Al Jarreau's "Black and Blues" is spot on.

Through research and reading a very helpful scholarly master's thesis entitled "An Oral History of Marching Band Traditions at Historically Black Colleges and Universities" written by Claire Millburn[2], I was able to find the origins of the Fifth Quarter. There are many different accounts and multiple stories, but what is for certain in all of the differing accounts, they all center around this one game in particular. The game was Alcorn

---

[2] Milliburn, Claire, *An Oral History of Marching Band Traditions at Historically Black Colleges and Universities* (2019). LSU Master's Thesis. 4906.

State University vs. Southern University which took place in Lorman, MS, on October 21st, 1972. According to Lawrence Jackson, a former director of bands at Southern University and a then student at SU at the time, back then, after a game, the home teams band would stay after the game and play the schools alma mater, and when that was done everyone left the stadium. Alcorn played their school's alma mater that day, and Southern University suddenly started playing, interrupting Alcorn's sacred alma mater.

So, the bands went back and forth. SU had a deeper music book, and eventually, after hours of exhausting musical warfare, Alcorn ran out of music, and someone sent a student back to the band room and the school's library to bring back sheet music with more songs. They handed them out in the stands and continued to play, and the two schools battled back and forth well into the dark Lorman, MS, star-filled sky. And so, the Fifth Quarter was born on this night in Mississippi.

The Zero Quarter originated in Jackson, MS. In 1997, Southern came to Jackson, MS, to play the Tigers of JSU. The Human Jukebox arrived at the Vet super early with the sole purpose of interrupting Jackson State's famous "Get Ready" entrance. As JSU marched in, SU was already seated in the stands and sat quietly until JSU approached them. SU waited until they were directly over The Boom and let them have it. Elongated to the limit, they marched shoulder to shoulder around the perimeter of the stadium headed to the ramp. Being stretched so thin in the limited space, The Boom was overpowered and could not keep a step or hear one another. So, they were directed to run to their seats, and once situated in the stands, it was on, and the Zero Quarter was born. SU's director of Bands, Dr. Isaac Greggs, loved to brag and show up opponents. This attack was his brainchild. The next year when JSU traveled to SU this time, The BOOM got there super early and repaid the favor by blowing Southern out, forcing Southern this time to run for their seats, and it was on once more. One more time, three years in a row, and this made it official, and now the Zero Quarter was a tradition people would look forward to as well. And so, the Zero Quarter was born in Jackson, MS.

Talladega College in Alabama has a wonderful marching band; A band that took social media by storm. They perform all over the country by request and heavy demand. The thing is, though, Talladega College does not have a football team. The Talladega College "the Great Tornado" Marching Band is cold-blooded, and I love to see and hear them in person whenever I can. Even though they do not have a football team, I get it. And I love it. See you at the Honda. And the band played on.

CHAPTER 8

WAVEE DAVE

"When I'm on stage, I am trying to do one thing: bring people joy."

- James Brown

Often in life, one is asked to reflect on those they admire. That person can be admired from a personal relationship and with analysis fueled by personal account. Other times that person can be admired from afar. Nevertheless, to explain why those individuals, in particular, have had such an impact on you, it's required that you paint a picture so that those unfamiliar with this particular individual can understand. Often, I am asked to "Name ten or so men or women who have earned your admiration and why them." On my list of such persons, there are the usual suspects. Persons who display or in the past have displayed excellence in their chosen field or fields of endeavor. Persons whose handling of both triumph and tragedy, success and misfortune provide lessons upon which a student of that particular individual or individuals can gain from. On my list are, in the majority, those individuals that you would expect. Included are my parents, my favorite political activists, football coaches, my favorite musician, artist, philosopher, writer, my favorite ball player and prize fighter, and so on.

However, one individual appears on my list of admired persons who always need some explanation. The others I mention need none, such as the great Muhammad Ali, Huey P. Newton, Marcus Garvey, Harriet Tubman, etc.

That individual I usually have to explain to the questioner is a man named David Chambers, affectionately known as Wavee Dave. People will respond, "Who was he?" or "What did he do?" I respond simply that he was a college mascot for Jackson State University. But to stop there would be the same as responding that Muhammed Ali was just a boxer, or Harriet Tubman was just a runaway slave, or Huey P. Newton was just a radical, or James Brown was just a dancer and entertainer, or Dr. King was just a preacher. A simple answer does a great disservice to not only the memory of the individual, but it also does a disservice to the person asking the question in terms of their proper understanding of who that individual actually was, was about, and meant in the grand universal scheme of things and how he has positively impacted the lives of thousands. This humble explanation is my effort to inform the reader and preserve the memory of a man who dedicated his whole adult life to bringing joy to thousands each week. He was indeed much more than just a college mascot.

Wavee Dave was a genius, a super star of immeasurable brilliance. Sent to a southern Black community desperately in need of a hero, and one they could count on to perform in the clutch when the chips were down and take their minds off of the poverty, racism, and socio-economic driven self-esteem issues that were a by-product of the deepest oppression fostered for generations. He was not just a mascot. He was a teacher, a scholar, a coach, an entertainer, an acrobat, a dancer, a unicyclist, a fighter, a tough guy, and an inspiration, and more appropriately, the greatest mascot of all times. One of the greatest human beings ever to visit our planet. The

G.O.A.T. A real badass too. A memory that can never be allowed to die.

Wavee Dave was part acrobat, part James Brown slash M.C. Hammer. He could easily out dance, out flip, and entertain any mascot foolish enough to step on the same football field with him. And I mean, he was a badass. He believed that what he was doing once he put on that Tiger suit was a divine mission; a mission given to him by God. If there was another mascot on the field with him and that mascot attempted to disturb him while he was on his post and about the business of entertaining God's people, the penalty would be severe. Fact is Wavee Dave would kick a mascot's ass in the blink of an eye. I witnessed these beat downs over and over again. Eventually, the word got out, you do not mess with the Tiger from Jackson State. The Mississippi Valley State Delta Devil, The Grambling State Tiger on more than one occasion, the University of Southern Mississippi Golden Eagle, the Alabama State Hornet, and the Northeastern Louisiana State Demon all fell to the fistic fury of one Wavee Dave, and I witnessed them all.

I've even heard about other beatdowns during road games that we could not attend. I do not know his official beat-down record, but I do know that he was undefeated. I vividly remember seeing other mascots slink away in shame and out of public view after being soundly beaten in a dance-off or a backflip exercise. "Hey, where did that other Tiger go?" It was dominance and a reign of terror that lasted well over twenty-plus years. Veteran mascots who had experienced Wavee before often stayed away from him. As far away from him as possible, they were usually standing as close as they could to a policeman or security guard or, better yet, near an exit, just in case Wavee got that feeling that he needed to mark his territory.

A native of Chicago, Illinois, David Chambers came to Jackson, Mississippi, in the early 1980s on a scholarship to march in the Sonic Boom of the South. He played the saxophone and displayed excellence in musicianship as well, earning his way to being section leader. Upon graduation and no longer able to march in the Boom, David needed something to do to support his postgraduate education as well as provide an outlet for all of that legendary energy and spirit. The past JSU tiger mascot had also graduated, and the opportunity to fill his shoes was offered to him. The rest, as they say, is history. For the next twenty-plus years, Wavee Dave, the alter ego of Mr. David Chambers, would be a fixture of iconic status at all JSU football and basketball games. His performance at basketball games was the stuff of legends as well, restricted only by the size of the arena floor as opposed to a 100 plus yard football field.

The SWAC treated him like royalty, and he was a superstar when visiting other SWAC and HBCU campuses for ball games. He was asked about as much as the quarterback or star point guard. Wavee was in demand and was a recognized and necessary fixture that had become an institution that was absolutely vital to the cultural experience sought by all that attended these games. Some indeed came just to see him. Wavee had become quite famous across the HBCU sporting diaspora while being featured on an old 1990's BET commercial promoting Black College football games featured on Saturday afternoons and Saturday evenings. The commercial featured Wavee running at full speed across the field and plowing headfirst into the goal post, leaving the goal post shaking afterward like it was the victim of a massive earthquake. This was a trick all Jackson State fans were very familiar with, but the nation was now intrigued by this stunt, and on BET, during game coverage that featured the JSU football teams, he got as much camera coverage as the head coaches.

His virtuoso performances thoroughly entertained the throngs of people gathered, and he was indeed a creative genius expanding the idea of what was expected of a college mascot. No longer could a mascot just stand there doing nothing for four quarters besides wearing the mascot suit of their school. They had to produce at least while sharing the field with Wavee, or your mascot and school would be embarrassed to no end. Wavee was often the subject of water cooler talk instead of the running back, or exciting kick returned for a touchdown to open the game.

In between plays or following being featured during The Boom's halftime performance, he would interact with fans of all ages in the stands. I once saw him sit in the laps of some old ladies, and they were reacting as if it were Billy Dee Williams or somebody of that nature. He was a movie star. Schools across the SWAC expected to see him when the Tigers came to town, and he delivered for them each and every time. Leaving those fan bases talking until the next time they got a chance to see him.

I once remember JSU losing a game to Tennessee State University. While leaving the game, a Tennessee State fan said, "We got y'all this time, my friend, but that Tiger y'all got is still undefeated." Wavee's arrival into a stadium was often atop a unicycle that he could ride with the speed, quickness, and skill of an expert unicyclist. He did not just hobble around with it, but instead, he rode the hell out of that thing. A member of Kappa Alpha Psi, riding that unicycle was a skill developed while pledging during his undergraduate years. He was often made to ride that unicycle to class and all over campus as part of his pledge process. Like with all things he engaged in, he mastered it and then had the brilliant idea to incorporate that unicycle into his arsenal of game-time entertainment.

In 2001, I took a picture of Wavee riding his unicycle on campus before the 2001 Alcorn game and a few years later posted it on social media when Facebook became a big thing. If you google search Wavee Dave on the images icon, you will undoubtedly see it. It has been used tons of times in articles and stories done on his life and legacy. Used in an official capacity on school websites as well. I'm very proud of that photo, and I still have the original.

Along the way, the Baby Tigers developed as a lasting legacy to Wavee's memory. Wavee would select area kids and kids from the community to perform with him during halftime. He would teach them dance routines and acrobatics that wowed and entertained Tiger fans for decades. He also demanded a certain expectation of those kids in the classroom, and if they wanted to perform, they had to engage in study hall before practice and produce their report cards for his approval or disapproval before making his selection on who would accompany him on road trips. Road trips that he often paid for out of his own pocket. They had little tiger suits of their own, and if a parent could not afford to pay for their child's suit, he would once again come out of his own pocket to make sure that child was dressed just like all of the others. A scholarship has been officially established in his name, and a street has been named after him on campus at Jackson State University, along with numerous trophies, plaques, and awards. Proclamations from the mayor, governor, and state legislators and even an Official Wavee Dave "Day" were commemorated.

Wavee Dave's contributions to JSU and Jackson, MS, are too numerous to count. My fondest memory of Wavee Dave came during a road trip my father took my sister and me on along with the Blue Bengals Association. One morning while still dark out, we left home for campus and boarded a bus along with my Uncle Amos and Uncle Howard to see the Tigers play in the Division I-AA playoffs in 1988 against the Stephen F. Austin Lumberjacks. While headed to Nacogdoches, Texas, for the game, the bus driver and others noticed what appeared to be the JSU Cheerleading Squad stranded on the side of the road having obvious vehicle difficulty. The bus stopped, and the JSU Cheerleaders boarded our bus to thunderous applause. I had never seen Wavee outside of his Tiger suit and did not know what he looked like at that point in my 12 years on the planet. There was a young man with them, and he stood out to me because of his Dwayne Wayne flip glasses and his brown leather aviator's jacket. Then My Uncle Howard asked my sister and me if we knew who this young man was, and we responded no. When my Uncle Howard explained to us that this young man was indeed none other than the Tiger, Wavee Dave, we cheered enthusiastically, and Wavee gave us each a high five and sat down near us, entertaining us for a great portion of that road trip to Nacogdoches, TX.

Wavee did not have to do that. But like I stated earlier, he felt that he was given a mission from God to dawn that Tiger suit and bring joy to as many as he could while he was on this earth. And that is what he did 24 hours a day, 365 days a year.

On December 21st, 2006, David "Wavee Dave" Chambers died of complications from kidney failure, becoming an ancestor in the African Ways of Knowing tradition. He indeed lived a life of adventure and served God's purpose for his life and indeed discovered the purpose for God, having allowed him time on this Earth, and he knocked it out of the park. Rest in Power and Godspeed. He was the undisputed Greatest of All Times, the King of the Cats, the Mack of the SWAC, and the champion of all halftime acts. The incomparable David "Wavee Dave" Chambers.

CHAPTER 9

LIBATIONS AND WAYS OF REMEMBERING

*"He who drinks wine without
libation is a traitor to the gods."*
- African proverb

The first Historically Black Colleges and Universities were largely established through the efforts of Black Churches and the support of American Missionary Associations along with the Freedmen's Bureau. Eventually, the 2nd Morrill Act, written in the year 1890, required the states, primarily the former Confederate States, to provide land grants for potential institutions dedicated for the establishment of Black Colleges. These new schools were for the education of newly freed slaves and their children. That is, if enrollment was denied to them by white colleges and universities in those states.

Certainly, following the Civil War, those white institutions did not allow Black students into their schools and violently defended them against Black educators and Black students. Thus, the Morrill Act of 1890 made it possible for the establishment of what we now refer to as HBCUs in the South. I discussed the first of these three, not ironically, that were established pre-Civil War and in Northern States. Cheyney, the first Higher Education Institution for Blacks in this country, was established in Pennsylvania and founded in 1837. Followed by two more, Lincoln University also established in the state of Pennsylvania and founded in 1854. Then Wilberforce University, established in the state of Ohio and founded in

1856. The first of those established post-Civil War was Shaw University, established in Raleigh, North Carolina, founded in 1865. Others quickly followed, such as Talladega College in the state of Alabama, Howard University in this nation's capital of Washington, D.C., Morehouse College in Atlanta, Georgia, Fisk University in Nashville, Tennessee, and Hampton Institute established in the State of Virginia.

Mississippi has a rich and powerful tradition of Historically Black Colleges and Universities. Many are still with us, and many have gone away not able to properly defend themselves against the racist and powerfully oppressive machine of Mississippi's legendary Jim Crow rule. And most of those no longer with us had at one time thriving football programs. There are those that are still with us, and their survival under these circumstances is worthy of tribute in and of itself. But some of these lost their football programs due to the financial strain and racism of the day that made the financial and physical cost just too much to bear in order to maintain them. Tougaloo College, for example, was founded in 1869 with help from The American Missionary Association of New York who bought 500 acres of what was one of the largest slave plantations in central Mississippi for the education of Freedmen and their children. Tougaloo, a stone's throw from Jackson, MS, housed in a neighboring town called Tougaloo, MS. Tougaloo is a Choctaw word that means "where two rivers cross," having quite the cultural connection with "High John The Conqueror," "Esu" and "Br'er Rabbit" who all met people at the crossroads in an African way of story-telling. During the Civil Rights era, Tougaloo was a powerhouse of radical thought and a favorite destination for Stockley Carmichael, who regularly organized students attending classes there for the battle raging for justice and human dignity in Mississippi.

Tougaloo College produced the "Tougaloo Nine," who set Mississippi afire with youthful ambitions of freedom. "We want justice now and not later," thought and activity were rampant. Tougaloo College also produced giants of the Mississippi fight for freedom, such as Lawrence Guyot, a 1963 graduate and director of The Mississippi Freedom Democratic Party, Joyce Ladner, Ph.D. and 1964 graduate who was a formidable sociologist who wrote a book called "The Death of White Sociology" which I read while attending Lane College, a small private HBCU located in Jackson, TN. Dr. Ladner also would become the first female president of Howard University. The Tougaloo College Bulldogs produced the great author Anne Moody and civil rights activist Ruben V. Anderson, a 1965 graduate and the first Black judge to sit on the Mississippi Supreme Court. Also, Constance Slaughter-Harvey, a 1967 graduate and the first Black judge in the State of Mississippi. The Bulldogs could also play a little football.

My research could track down only a few accounts of their football past, but I was very interested and able to see how they fared versus Jackson State back in the day. The Bulldogs and Tigers did battle several times during the 1920s through the 1960s. The Tougaloo College, Jackson State game at one time was quite a happening. I know that the Bulldogs and Tigers at one time played an annual Thanksgiving Day Classic, and they considered each other rivals due to the close proximity of the two schools. Before 1946, records are sketchy for a number of reasons, but I was able to find an old newspaper clipping that references this Classic being played in 1929, resulting in a victory for the Tigers 19-0. In 1930, the Bulldogs were the victors 29-6. Followed by ties in 1931 and 1932. During the season of 1930, The Bulldogs won its first and only Championship, winning the SCAC title that year. Records are much better by 1946, and the Tigers would dominate, with the Bulldogs winning the only victory that I could find during that stretch of 2-0 in 1947. In 1961, Tougaloo College was forced to discontinue the football program due to financial stresses too much to withstand.

Rust College, located in Holly Springs, Mississippi, was founded in 1866, making it the 2nd oldest private college in the state. Rust College is one of the only ten Historically Black Colleges and Universities founded before 1868 whose doors are still open to students seeking higher education. Rust College also has a rich history of producing giants such as the great Ida B. Wells, writer, and freedom fighting radical of the highest regards; Leslie B. Mclemore, civil rights activist and once interim mayor of Jackson, Mississippi; journalist Clinton LeSueur and once congressional candidate; and Perry Wilbon Howard, attorney, and once assistant U.S. attorney general. Rust College could also play a little football, fielding very good ball clubs at one time. The Rust College Bearcats also played the Tigers of Jackson State several times that I could find through my research. They squared off many times in the 1940s, 1950s, 1960s.

As with Tougaloo College and sadly, most Historically Black College and Universities records were not kept in some cases, and some records were destroyed in fires and floods. So, you will notice that many records usually got much better by the 1940s, when a more concerted effort was made to preserve records more academically. So, I have no way of knowing how many times Rust College and Tougaloo played Jackson State. But in the several battles, I could find waged between the Tigers of Jackson State and the Bearcats of Rust College, the Bearcats were only able to defeat the Tigers of JSU only once back in 1947. Given the limited records on the game that I could find, however, it does not mean that it was the only time, just the only one I dug up evidence of. Ironically, like the Tougaloo score the year prior in 1947, that victory against the Tigers of JSU in 1948 ended in a score of 2-0, giving the Bearcats their only apparent victory against JSU. Rust College's most notable football player was Eddie Smith, who, once finished with his playing career at Rust College, would become the first Black man elected Mayor of Holly Springs, Mississippi. Rust College was forced to end its football program following the conclusion of the 1965 football season.

Coahoma Community College, located in Clarksdale, MS. Famous for being the home of blues pioneer Robert Johnson and being the birthplace of the blues, was established in 1924 and still fighting the good fight and fielding football teams.

Mary Holmes College, an HBCU founded to educate Black women in 1892, was located in West Point, Mississippi, and came to its end during the year 2005. Mississippi Industrial College, an HBCU founded in Holly Springs, Mississippi, in 1905, was established by The Colored Methodist Episcopal Church just as my alma mater Lane College was. And in fact, Mississippi Industrial College's records and transcripts are kept on the campus of Lane College in Jackson, TN. In 1982, the campus of

Mississippi Industrial College closed its doors. Mississippi Industrial College's football team was able with limited resources to produce Jim Thomas, who went on to play Canadian League Football and was named an All-Star during the 1963 season. Also, they produced Robert Ledbetter, who became a great high school football head coach who would go on to coach at Norfolk State University, the New Orleans Saints, the New York Giants, and the New York Jets. Also, the tiny college produced the likes of Osborne Bell, a 1963 Graduate who became the first Black elected sheriff of Marshall County, Mississippi, post Reconstruction. Elias Cottrell, born into slavery in 1853, became the Mississippi Industrial College's Founder and 7th Bishop of the CME Church, elected to that position in 1894. And for that life that lived from slavery to freedom, these histories must be remembered, shared, and told repeatedly. Future generations must be armed with the knowledge of what their ancestors have done to fill the current and future generations and fill them with the passion necessary not just to survive but to thrive and win. Libations throughout the African Diaspora for all of our ancestors who lived, fought, and died so that I could one day pick up a pen and know how to use it.

Not only in Mississippi but all over, the HBCU sporting diaspora stories worthy of remembrance can be found that need to be shared. For instance, Jack Roosevelt Robinson, once a standout tailback for the UCLA Bruins, played in an all-black backfield featuring Kenny Washington and Woody Strode. They all would become just as legendary in their chosen fields of endeavor as Jackie Robinson. Before Robinson ever tried his hand at the game of baseball, his stellar college football career was interrupted by World War II. He played in the Negro

Leagues and later became the first Black man to integrate Major League Baseball in 1947, playing with the Brooklyn Dodgers eventually being enshrined into Professional Baseball's Hall of Fame, which is amazing considering he had not previously played the game of baseball in his life. Most do not know that once home from the war, Jackie Robinson had been such a respected football player for UCLA. He was offered the vacant head football coaching position at HBCU Samuel Huston College, now Huston-Tillotson University, which he accepted.

An original member institution of the SWAC, Samuel Huston College's football program was led by future Negro League and Major League Baseball Hall of Famer Jackie Robinson for two years until the strain of financial woes forced the school to end its football program. How many know that tidbit of information? How many feel that more should? If you do, these stories won't be preserved if we do not learn them and learn to tell them. Libations. Going back to fetch it. Ways of remembering.

CHAPTER 10

JACK, DEACON, CHARLES & FREDRICK

"There are all kinds of smiles. On the football field, I mostly used the one where the hawk spots the dove."

- Deacon Jones

My passion for African American history is so strong that I sometimes feel the presence of the subjects that I study. Currently, there are four men on my mind, so I get the feeling that I need to touch on them. I think they may be communicating the message "tell them about us."

John Robert "Jack" Spinks is a legend in the lore of Alcorn State. When Jack first walked onto the campus of Alcorn at six feet and 230 pounds, he was harassed by the coaches to give football a try. Interested, he did and blew their doors off with literally no playing experience. At his size, which was huge then, he was made a guard. He was great at opening holes for the team's running backs. Jack had such incredible speed that he was switched to the fullback position. So, his first start came as a freshman, and ironically the first football game that he ever saw was the very first game that he played in. Jack Spinks became the first football player from the state of Mississippi to be drafted into the NFL. The Pittsburgh Steelers drafted him in 1952. He also played with the Chicago Bears in 1953, the Green Bay Packers from 1955 to 1956, and the New York Giants from 1956 to 1957. The legacy of John Robert "Jack" Spinks is forever cast in stone. The stadium on campus where Alcorn State plays was named in honor of the man that was more likely to run you over even though his blazing speed could blow by everyone. While playing with the Green Bay Packers, he was switched back to the guard position because he was told that the team would not keep three fullbacks. Jack thrived yet again, not missing a beat, and the only thing that changed was his jersey number.

David D. "Deacon" Jones was from Eatonville, Florida, and grew up wanting to be a Florida A&M Rattler. When he got to the campus, he was told by legendary Coach Jake Gaither that he was not good enough to play there. So, he was offered a scholarship with the South Carolina Bulldogs, an HBCU MEAC powerhouse. Unfortunately, his scholarship was taken from him, and he was kicked out of school for participating in a sit-in at Woolworth's lunch counter in South Carolina protesting Jim Crow segregation laws in the state. Ironically around the same time, one of the assistant coaches there got offered a head coaching job at then Mississippi Vocational College, later named Mississippi Valley State University in 1974. Deacon got to campus and immediately made an impact being the first defensive lineman to register 100 tackles in one season, a feat usually the domain of much lighter and swifter linebackers. The Los Angeles Rams drafted deacon in 1961.

Unfortunately as well, the NFL did not keep statistics on tackling a quarterback in the backfield. At the time, such a play was counted as the same as any other tackle. Deacon made a career of this. It was his niche. He began to hate quarterbacks and once stated that he wanted to put all quarterbacks in a big sack and beat the hell out of it with a baseball bat. Tackling the quarterback in the backfield because of him became known as sacking the quarterback. Deacon was also notorious for using his big hands to slap an offensive lineman who was attempting to block him right in the earhole. This move became an illegal tactic in later years. Because the NFL started keeping statistics on sacking the quarterback so late in his career, it is estimated that Deacon has at least 50 more sacks than the NFL's current leading sacker Bruce Smith who has a registered 200 sacks.

Renowned as the older brother of civil rights icon Medgar Evers, Charles Evers was a star center for the Alcorn State Braves. His younger brother Medgar was a star halfback. Charles Evers, admittedly, was not as talented as Medgar. He compensated by being tough, nasty, and as mean as possible. He would step on hands in an era where cleats were made of metal and kick players down and gauge at eyes. Later, Charles would move to Chicago and become a big-time numbers runner and policy wheel operator who owned clubs, restaurants, and a brothel or two. Although gangster, the money he was making was used to finance Medgar's efforts as field secretary for the NAACP in the state of Mississippi. The NAACP National office gave Medgar little support as well as very little financial backing. Charles' income from his activities in Chicago was almost solely responsible for keeping Medgar's movement afloat. Charles had legendary battles with Chicago's Italian mob and, with the help of his buddy from Yazoo, Mississippi, were oftentimes successful in defending their business interests against them. When Medgar was assassinated, Charles jumped on an airplane with a shotgun and two .45's, in a day when you could do that, with the sole purpose of finding Medgar's killer Byron

De La Beckwith. Fortunately, he never found him and decided to take Medgar's place in the fight for freedom in the state of Mississippi. Charles Evers would go down in history as the first black man elected mayor in a Mississippi town post Reconstruction. Once asked by a reporter if he was worried about white vigilantes shooting at participants during an upcoming protest as had been the case in neighboring states, Mr. Evers responded clearly, calmly, and with authority, "This is Mississippi, we shoot back."

Although not from Mississippi, this young man's story bears telling primarily because of its historical significance and because he holds a significant place in my personal pantheon of my favorite revolutionary activists. Frederick Douglass Kirkpatrick was born in 1933 in Haynesville, Louisiana. He went on to play football for four years under the leadership and guidance of the great coach Eddie Robinson. After a stellar four-year career at Grambling State University, then Grambling State College, he had a brief professional football career that ended early due to a knee injury. He, along with Buddy Earnest "Chilli Willie" Thomas, founded an organization called the Deacons for Defense and Justice in 1964. Kirkpatrick would return to Grambling to speak with Coach Eddie Robinson to gain his support and influence within the state to help the group. Robinson, whose words to Kirkpatrick which he has never shared, probably led to behind the scenes support but Coach Robinson could not in those turbulent times show outward support to such an organization and expect not to receive a backlash from government officials, especially when his school relied on the state for much of his financial support. Kirkpatrick and his Deacons for Defense would often physically protect marchers in the state of Mississippi and once were even requested by the Reverend Dr. Martin Luther King, Jr. to protect nonviolent protesters in such a march. Charles Evers had said that Dr. King stayed at his home several times when coming to the state of Mississippi. When he asked him one day why he liked staying with him so much, Charles said that King replied, it's because you have all those goons out there protecting the house.

These four gentlemen aren't as talked about as say a Jerry Rice or Walter Payton, but their lives played just as vital a role in forging ahead in the fight for justice and freedom in the state of Mississippi and the examples of manhood they put on display. These men must be just as remembered, just as talked about, so that their memories can never be erased as many would like for them to be. And to know that the greatest wide receiver, the greatest tailback, and the greatest defensive lineman of all times were produced by tiny black colleges in the state of Mississippi is of note and a story worthy to be told.

** Of course, the tailback was Jackson State University's, Walter Payton.

CHAPTER 11

THE 1970'S AND THE TURBULENCE IT PRODUCED IN THE STATE

"Free the Land!!!"
- Republic of New Afrika

At the tail end of the 1960s heading into the decade of the 1970s, the Mississippi SWAC schools were as strong as ever, especially Alcorn State and Jackson State. In 1968 Alcorn State tied with Grambling State for the SWAC Championship. In 1969, Alcorn State won the SWAC title outright. Alcorn was again the undisputed champion of the SWAC and repeated that feat again in 1970. The Tigers of Jackson State would go on a tremendous campaign, winning a share of the SWAC Championship with Co-Champions Grambling State in 1971, 1972, and 1973. Alcorn State won a share of the SWAC title again and shared it again with Grambling State. Alcorn State would win it outright again in 1976 and capture a share of it once more, sharing the title with Eddie Robinson's dominant G-Men.

Arkansas-Pine Bluff, Grambling State, Southern, and Texas Southern would share an unusual four-way tie as Co-SWAC Champions in 1966. A few months before that, on June 16th, 1966, in Greenwood, Mississippi, Stockley Carmichael gave the speech that would cement his legacy forever. Stockley said to those gathered that hot June night in 1966, "We been saying freedom for six years, what we are going to start saying now is Black Power." And so, a new generation of the descendants of Mother Africa had stated their position on the matter never to be forgotten forevermore.

Other radical actions in response to the savagery of Jim Crow Mississippi were filling the streets also at this historical time period. On Friday, May 15th, 1970, city and state police would attack approximately 100 African American students attending Jackson State College, now Jackson State University. As a result of the city and state police's actions, the attack on the students resulted in the deaths of two of them, Jackson State Junior, Phillip Gibbs, 21 years of age, and Jim Hill high school student James Earl Green, 17 years old, who was walking home from work. This attack also caused the serious bodily injury of eleven more students. The bullets that riddled the buildings of the J-State campus are still there as a constant reminder to all. For context, the students were protesting because they had had enough white citizens driving through campus, using it as a main thoroughfare to downtown.

Often students would be struck by automobiles, and of course, the white drivers never stopped. Often it was suspected that these acts were purposeful and sort of a sport to these depraved white citizens of the State. The whites driving through often threw bricks and rocks at both male and female students walking to class, shouting sexually inappropriate and vulgar comments to Jackson States female students and faculty. After such an event on May 14th, 1970, a white man drove through shouting that he had just killed Charles Evers and the students went after him. Soon the full power of the state's racist law enforcement organizations filled with card-carrying members of the Ku Klux Klan and various other white supremacist groups marched on the campus. After midnight, on May 15th,

1970, the city and state police said they heard a gunshot and ruthlessly unloaded bullets on dormitories, shooting into lobbies and windows, killing two and injuring eleven. For safety concerns, Jackson State University President John A. Peoples canceled classes for the rest of the semester, and the class of 1970 was sadly deprived of a commencement ceremony.

In 1971, as Jackson State was about to report to camp for the 1971 football season, more unrest would unfold. On an August morning in 1971, the FBI and Jackson Police, in cooperation and without search warrants, stormed a home not far from the Jackson State campus on 1148 Lewis Street. The humble home was the headquarters of an organization called the Republic of New Africa (RNA). This organization has its roots in Detroit, Michigan. The RNA, heavily influenced by the teaching of Malcolm X, believed that the government owed reparations to the descendants of African enslaved persons who had never been compensated for their ancestors 400 years of free forced labor, enriching millions of white Americans and building the worlds' greatest so-called Democracy.

The Republic of New Africa had selected the former confederate states as their new provisional Government. The RNA selected Hinds County, Mississippi, as the new nation's capital and base. The RNA bought several acres of land, and when they came to claim it, they were interrupted by whites, mainly Klansmen, in an attempt to run them away—led by another Jackson, Mississippi legend and future Jackson, Mississippi mayor, Chokwe Lumumba, who was a brilliant attorney that had represented Tupac Shakur whom he had known since he was a child growing up in the movement. Successfully in court, Lumumba led armed Black men in a chant of "Free the Land," causing the cowardly whites to flee, freeing up the way for the RNA to take possession of the land they had legally paid for. Those present in the house raid on that August morning in 1971 were stripped, handcuffed, and marched through the streets tied at the neck and the ankles to one another in a scene so reminiscent of the days most of white Mississippi had desperately wanted to return.

Many were imprisoned for decades and forgotten by the outside world, but Black Mississippi never forgot, and this is one of the social factors contributing to Attorney Lumumba's successful bid for mayor. The people spoke, and the people won. After his mysterious death on February 25, 2014, the radical mayor's son Chockwe Antar Lumumba also won a successful bid for mayor, and once again, Black Jackson had shown up and showed out. The location of these events is one reason for its generally unknown status. Through a Black College football cultural framework, I believe these stories, even from the remotest of locations, can be more rigorously, adequately examined, and explored, including the academics on campus and the people in the community not interested in higher education and put them together in the study of our histories on a common plain of Blackness. Free the Land!!

CHAPTER 12

ORGANIZATIONAL THEORY: BLACK MISSISSIPPI'S TRADITION OF BENEVOLENCE & BROTHERHOOD

> *"Mobilization is not organization.*
> *This must be properly*
> *understood."*
> - Stokley Carmichael / Kwame` Ture

Necessity has always been the mother of invention. The African has created many unknown and unrecognized contributions to the civilized world, the greatest of which is civilization itself. Man's need for safety, shelter, knowledge, and education in a forbidding atmosphere full of dangers spurred on these glorious innovative and life-changing ingenuities. Engineering, architecture, science, math, medicine, and technology advanced the race (the human race). For which we have had to fight to rightfully claim as our own.

From the time of the inception of the transcontinental slave trade, the African, out of necessity, have had to band together in a strange land that was hell-bent on enslaving and dominating him mentally and, of course, physically. One way we accomplished this was to create our own fraternal orders and benevolent societies. Necessity called for us to go back and fetch it (Sankofa), our sense of tribalism in a newer form to accommodate or more appropriately combat our new hellish situation.

To this end, self-help and collective mutual aid, and brotherly assistance were the weapons of choice in the diaspora. Organizations such as The Twelve Knights and Daughters of Tabor were founded in 1846 as an anti-slavery society. The Underground Railroad or "Underground" was a way more intricate form of fraternalism than most research has provided the common student evidence of. Here are a few of these organizations: Prince Hall Freemasonry in 1775, the Ancient Egyptian Arabic Order Nobles of the Mystic Shrine in 1893, the Improved Benevolent Protective Order of Elks of the World in 1898, the Negro mutual benefit societies of Philadelphia in 1831, the Free African Society, Philadelphia in 1787, the New York African Society for Mutual Relief in 1808, the Black Sons of Ham or the United Sons of Ham of America in 1865, the Phoenix Society, New York City in 1833, Grand United Order of Odd Fellows in 1843, the Young Men's Literary and Mutual Reform Society, Pittsburgh in 1837, Coloured American Temperance Society, Philadelphia in 1831, the African Benevolent Society, Chillicothe, OH in 1827, Free Dark Men of Color, Charleston in 1791, Free African Union Society, Newport, RI in the 1780s, the Adelphic Union Library Association, Boston in 1836 and culminating with perhaps the most powerful of all The Universal Negro Improvement Association in 1914.

Many of the aforementioned Black associations, societies, and fraternal orders directly influenced another institution of African American reliance and pride, the Black Church. The African Methodist Episcopal Church was founded in 1816 under the extraordinary leadership of two men named Richard Allen and Absolom Jones. Clearly, these men and their followers knew exactly the

African-ness of their existence, but contrary to what most of us believe, this remarkable Black Religious experience was brought into fruition by Allen and Jones from the assistance and aid of yet another Black society they both belonged to, The Philadelphia Free African Society which these two genius men were the co-leadership of. Often neglected in reflection of the Black Churches role in the fight for civil rights for Black Americans was the role of Black fraternal organizations and Black benevolent societies. These organizations kept secrets out of necessity because membership was dangerous in a society that did not want Africans to congregate for any other purpose than working and doing the heavy lifting and burden-bearing for the white citizens of the quote new world.

These organizations provided infrastructure that prepared Blacks with exposure and use of certain levels of cultural sophistication and skills taught in the house away from the glaring eye of the oppressor class. Many of these associations had elections and positions both elected and appointed, such as president, vice president, secretary, field marshal, major general, potentate, exalted ruler, historian, and other officers. Financial responsibility, brotherhood, racial pride, and education were qualities held in high regard and taught voraciously through officer and membership training. Burial insurance to say goodbye respectfully and tastefully to loved ones and financial loans for housing at a time when no bank would loan to Blacks was invaluable. These stories provided proof of collective responsibility and collective group economics and welfare work. Taking care of widows and orphans was a way of promoting manhood within the community.

In my opinion, the promotion of manhood and manly deeds, words, and actions were the greatest of virtues exposed to the African American community. This combated the constant barrage of reminders and treatment designed to enforce a sense of deserved belittlement and a sense of constant mental and physical states of boyhood. Moral obligation to your fellow brother and, by proxy, his family were tenants that carried an almost religious overtone. These societies, fraternal orders, and associations, more than any other factor in my opinion through the application of many and various forms, saw us through the difficulties of slavery, reconstruction, Jim Crow, and the first, second, and third waves of the Great Migration.

One organizational characteristic we seem to have lost along the way is the ability to overlook differences, both major and minor, for the collective good of the whole. For example, the Free African Society of Philadelphia, from its inception, chose purposefully to be non-denominational. It accepted free Blacks and religious persuasions. With the wisdom to recognize that there was safety in numbers and two was better than one, they were too few to make a foolish requirement to minimize membership and participation, such as having a specific religious denomination. The great Dr. W.E.B. Dubois stated in regards to the Free African Society that in 1787 "How great a step this was" and that "we of today scarcely realize."

CHAPTER 13

A MODERN CONCEPTUALIZATION

*"Black Power is giving power to
people who have not had the power
to determine their destiny."*
- Dr. Huey P. Newton

J. Edgar Hoover, the first director of the Federal Bureau of Investigation (F.B.I.), once stated that The Black Panther Party for Self Defense "was the greatest threat to the internal security of the United States." Those who oppress others become threatened when the victims of said oppression rise and take formal organizing steps to bring an end to their sufferings. The Black Panther Party for Self Defense was founded in Oakland, California, in 1966 by two young college students Huey P. Newton and Bobby Seale started complimentary breakfast and free lunch programs in the Black community long before the government-backed public school system did so. In fact, an argument can be made that the school system only did so to take credit away from the architects of this idea born of philosophy of feeding the community and people learning best through observation and participation. The Black Panther party also formed free clinics and ambulance services aimed at serving the health needs of a neglected community. The Panthers also provided education in the form of fully accredited schools with licensed teachers for the children of the membership to attend. When you do and accomplish things in your own self-interest, you become public enemy number one in the eyesight of the oppressor and his watchdogs tasked with keeping the slaves on the plantation and in full compliance.

In this case, J. Edgar Hoover and his government-backed COINTELPRO or Counter-Intelligence Program in operation from 1956 through 1971. Its purpose was a series of covert and, on many occasions, illegal surveillance, discrediting membership, and disturbing organizations well within their citizenship rights and guarantees. Written documentation produced by Hoover and his COINTELPRO aimed to "stop the rise of the Black Messiah."

As a member of several Black fraternal organizations, I personally feel ashamed that Mr. Hoover or someone like him never made the same comments concerning our collegiate African American Fraternity and Sorority Greek letter organizations. Once involved in civil rights to a degree that perhaps will never be fully explored. Today the question must be asked, what are we really doing? Seriously? We talk a good game, and as big and bad as we claim to be, and indeed we once were, what are we doing? Where are our banks, where are our hospitals, our schools? I am a proud member of Alpha Phi Alpha Fraternity Incorporated, I am a Prince Hall Mason, Prince Hall Shriner, and an Elk, but I have often wondered these things while engaged in various community service projects.

It would seem that we are only scratching the surface of our full potential. We are all proud of our various memberships and accomplishments, but how can we instill that same sort of call to action. Sure, maintaining organizational traditions passed down through the years but outside of a few community service projects, although very meaningful, lacking in the power and inspiration it once carried. Often when called to action, we are merely going through the motions, ritual, and dogma without seeing the visionary reasons for the creation of those projects in the first place. We need to return to pledge mode and begin to mobilize ourselves into squadrons ready to be deployed into battle against ignorance, poverty, sickness, hunger, and of course, oppression. The Panhellenic Council is a sleeping giant. We are small collectively but mighty together when we stand as one unified and qualified to resurrect a community from its present condition. Either that or we are just a bunch of paraphernalia wearers.

The very moment we were granted the right of full integration, all of our businesses started to close and disappear almost overnight. That was the fate of our hotels, restaurants, movie theaters, motels, and hotels. And the most hurtful was what a negative effect integration had on our Historically Black Colleges and Universities. We pioneered and championed our people in a post Reconstruction period and beyond. From our ranks came the civil rights leader and common foot soldiers alike. Let us not drop the baton of seeming to be the shining knights that routinely do the impossible. The old guard would be ashamed, I feel. We are two million and a half strong. If we all donated a dollar each earmarked for the construction of a building for the purpose of our choosing as starters, our version of the Pentagon with our version of joint chiefs meeting there regularly. Think of the possibilities of fifty dollars each or one hundred dollars each or one thousand each. There are socio-economic problems, educational deficits, drug and prostitution problems, and health concerns we could tackle head-on on our own. That is power.

We hear a lot these days about bipartisanship splitting the country in half. The same can be said for us. Sure, competition and rivalry can be healthy and fun too, however, we cannot refuse to work together due to varying affiliations in a modern context. That would be breaking the first and most important rule of The Free African Society back in 1787. Let us learn from our past. You had to be of a certain elk in the classroom to be accepted into these organizations of ours or of a certain standing in the community to be allowed the opportunity to join. We are too smart and hardworking, especially collectively, not to take control of our own destinies and the destinies of our community's welfare again.

Medgar Evers, the great freedom fighter, and his older brother Charles Evers were quintessential exponents of the idea of fraternal and mutual aid and brotherhood. Both belonged to multiple organizations that exposed the importance of Black manhood, brotherhood, and collective group protection. Medgar Evers himself was a Prince Hall Mason, Prince Hall Shriner, a member of the Improved Benevolent Protective Order of Elks of the World {I.B.P.E.O.W.), and the N.A.A.C.P. Evers' employed these groups to provide meeting spaces for civil rights planning and strategy meetings. Slain in the driveway of his home by a coward in front of his family, Evers, was the dictionary definition of a man. Evers was dressed in Elk regalia inside of his coffin by members of the I.B.P.O.E.W. I am sure by his own request to serve as a constant example. Medgar's brother Charles Evers had some of the same affiliations along with a few other more secret clandestine affiliations. Leading the fight for racial equality in Mississippi following the death of his brother, Charles joined-together with men like Rudy Shields to create a secret organization called 'THE ENFORCERS' whose duty it was to protect the life of Evers' and an even more secret group of young men assembled at the behest of Rudy Shields called 'THE SPIRIT' whose duty it was to enforce boycotts, and you did not want 'THE SPIRIT' to come to visit you at night!' This group was established to physically protect him and others like him from white mob violence in the state. Remarkably, when you study the amount of violence waged against Blacks in the state, it's amazing to see the amount of courage that the Evers men exuded during the height of Jim Crow.

The organizational affiliations they shared combined with a sense of deserved manhood provided them the will and partnership to protect themselves and discourage violence by way of returning violence once attacked. Charles Evers ran for mayor in Fayette County, Mississippi. Evers won the election, making him the first Black man to be elected mayor inside the state of Mississippi post-reconstruction. He could not have accomplished such an amazing feat of daring alone. Angry and embarrassed by the reality of a Black man now residing in the mayor's house, whites apart of the local government pulled out of office just quitting almost all at once, including the treasury department who before the abandoned their positions spent all of the counties' funds hoping to make the road ahead as difficult for the new Black Mayor as possible all the while painting a picture of incompetence and financial inability within his tenor in office from the beginning.

The Ancient Egyptian Arabic Order of the Nobles of the Mystic Shrine, commonly referred to as the Prince Hall Shriners, upon hearing of this dastardly deed by the whites in local government in Fayette county immediately drafted a supplementary report and gave it to the committee on charity and submitted a request to help their fellow brother out of this horrible predicament. The committee taking into account the greater good of the Black community and the implications of a successful mayoral tenor, asked the brotherhood for enough money to send Mayor Evers to allow him enough funds to cover the counties' governmental expenses providing him with the necessary capital needed to run the county for a year.

In the phenomenal scholarly work of Dr. Akinyele Omowale Umoja in his book 'WE WILL SHOT BACK," Dr. Umoja tells an amazing story of resistance born out of a necessity to protect the Black community from the violence of Jim Crow-era Mississippi heaped upon Blacks by the white citizens there who believed it their God-given right to terrorize people of color. The story goes as follows: On page 59, in chapter 3 entitled "CAN'T GIVE UP MY STUFF," Dr. Umoja writes: **"**MacArthur Cotton had been recruited by Moses in the summer of 1961. Cotton, a native of Attala County, had just finished his freshman year at Tougaloo College (near Jackson}. Cotton and other SNCC workers came to the Walthall municipality of Tylertown in 1961. Local people told Cotton and his comrades about "some of the old brothers" who prevented night riders from terrorizing a Black community outside of Tylertown. Nightriders had reportedly come across the bridge at Magee's Creek, which separated this Black community from the predominantly white neighborhoods of the city. To no avail, members of the Black community warned that the terrorism must stop. Local Blacks told Cotton that during a raid by nightriders, a group of 'brothers** with...ANCIENT CONNECTIONS' captured a white supremacist marauder. 'ANCIENT CONNECTIONS' suggested that the Black captors were part of a fraternal order. The nightriders' head was severed from his body and placed on the bridge as a warning to white terrorists. After this act of counterterrorism, no white person crossed the Magee's Creek bridge unless 'on business and treated {Black} people in a respectful manner. This Walthall County Black enclave served as a 'haven' for SNCC workers. As in the Black neighborhood in Danville, Virginia, which was protected by snipers, nonviolent activists could receive protection and refuge. The identification of haven communities for protection throughout the state was essential to SNCC's work in the state."

3

---

[3] Umosa, Akinyele Onowale *"We Will Shoot Back: Armed Resistance in the Mississippi Freedom Movement"* (2013) New York: New York University Press.

CHAPTER 14

C.O. CHINN / THE MAN, THE MYTH, THE LEGEND

> *"Every white man in that town knew you didn't fuck with C.O. Chinn. He'd kick your natural ass. "*
> - Mateo "Flukie" Suarez

There are men and women who have lived and died that have had such a glorious impact on the African diaspora, yet the mention of their names hardly raises an eyebrow. This can be attributed mostly to a concerted effort by those who control disseminating information to certain groups of people who do not control the very narrative they themselves create. Furthermore, we have a lack of producers of information on those who should be kept alive in the memory of people they represented, fought, and died for.

Ancestor veneration is a lasting key component of African-centered thinking. This practice is based on one very simple concept. The love and respect that one has for the deceased. Based primarily on the belief that someone who has passed away and has gone to join the realm of the ancestors has a continued existence so long as you continue to raise their names in tribute so that their actions and deeds are not lost to the generations that follow them that never knew them and would otherwise have never heard of them. This is the responsibility of the African-centered individual. Ancestors are alive when people remember them, they are alive when what they did or said inspires others to act in a positive and productive manner.

One such man whom I wish to make known to the community is a man by the name of C.O. CHINN or, in some circles, BADASS C.O. CHINN. In other cases, a fact often lost and skipped over purposely is the fact that the wonderful brothers and sisters that practiced non-violence were indeed backed up by wonderful brothers and sisters that were very violent in defense of them. This is why they lived, this is why they gained victories, and this is why they lived to tell their tales, but oftentimes forgetting to mention those brave men and women who provided them refuge and physical protection from a violent, crazed hateful society that quelled any notion of Black equality with murder, rape, and arson. C.O. Chinn was one of those men that did not back down from any force that challenged his manhood and his right to be a man. C.O. Chinn was not an unusual man in the Deep South. But he was an extraordinary individual that struck fear into the well-established Jim Crow system of governance. A pure individual. He was not beholden to any outside forces and answered to no one. He did and acted as he saw fit. The man who owned a 152-acre farm in Canton, MS. Chinn also owned one of Mississippi's most popular African American owned and operated night clubs, Canton, Mississippi's Club Desire. He was a successful entrepreneur to such a degree in my research, and every time I dig, I find some other avenue he used to generate capital so that he could remain his own man, financially beholden to no one. Chinn sometimes crossed the line into illegal business practices like his huge bootlegging operation, which he used to pay off the law. These payoffs allowed him the flexibility to operate without constant badgering from the police, and when faced with it, he acted like they meant nothing to him because he was often paying off their superiors. It is rumored that he was also a pimp that controlled a brothel or two. Although the fact that I cannot substantiate. Called fearless by those who knew him, Chinn came of age on a small family farm.

Chinn refused to work for white people. In fact, this is mainly how his reputation began. As an independent farmer early in adulthood, a white farmer disrespectfully approached his mother, saying that C.O. Chinn needed to be working for a white man in order to operate in this particular county in Mississippi or that he needed to pack up and leave the county or else. When the young Chinn learned of this once his mother delivered the message to him without hesitation, he went and grabbed his .38 caliber pistol and immediately found this very same white man, pointed the pistol in his face, and told him to stay out of CHINN family business or else he should be the one leaving the county if he wanted to remain on top of the ground as opposed to six feet under it.

Blacks who witnessed this event were shocked and filled with fear but also deep down a sense of pride that a Black man not only stood up for his mother and family and his right to be a man. To this community of Black people, he would from that point forward be known as BADASS C.O. CHINN. Whites who witnessed this event from that point moving forward would label him THAT CRAZY NIGGER C.O. CHINN.

Civil rights participants of note, such as CORE field secretary Mateo Suarez stated that "Every white man in that town knew you didn't fuck with C.O. Chinn. He'd kick your natural ass." Chinn had a blood feud, but one built on mutual respect or acknowledgment of mutual annihilation with the Madison County Sheriff and ex-Marine, one Billy Noble. The two men, one Black and one white, had an agreement that if he was called in to arrest Chinn, they would literally fistfight in the street, and if Chinn won the fight with the sheriff, he got to walk free. But if the Sheriff won the fight, he would put on the cuffs and haul Chinn to lock up. There were many of these fights over the years, sometimes Chinn won, and sometimes the Sheriff won. Sheriff Nobles, a very tough man who himself loved nothing more than a good fight, once stated, "there are only two bad sons of bitches in this county, me and that nigger C.O. Chinn."

Any other officer of the law who attempted to arrest Chinn was in for a good whoopin' or a bullet. Chinn did not allow any other officer to arrest him except the sheriff, contingent upon the fact that he could first whip him in a fistfight. One day in 1963, Chinn walked into a courtroom to show support for a young civil rights worker from up North who was arrested on a bogus charge. The problem was Chinn walked into the courtroom wearing his .38 holstered pistol around his waist. See, Chinn knew that he was not supposed to do that, that guns were not allowed in the courts. The judge, well aware of Chinn and his reputation, tried to level with him, a kindness that I'm almost certain that he would not have afforded to any other Black man. "You know you can't come in here wearing that gun," stated the judge. See, Chinn knew that the Sheriff was in that courtroom, and he was wearing his. Chinn stated to the judge, "As long as that son of a bitch is wearing his, I'm gonna keep mine." The judge, thinking all hell was about to break loose, stated, "Boys, boys, no. Why don't you put your guns on the table over here in front of the bench? Let's be good boys." Both men set their pistols down and stared at each other with looks that could kill. Whites who were absolutely notorious for the violence they reaped upon Blacks were indeed scared to death of C.O. Chinn. One of his lasting legacies is that he saved the lives of many civil rights workers and volunteers by his sheer presence. If Chinn was there, they all were safe.

Chinn's wife, Mamie Chinn, stated that "My husband was always fearless, my husband never been no nonviolent man. He'd fight the devil out of hell if he had to." Chinn taught his children to work hard, treat everyone right, respect everybody but take no mess off nobody, regardless of color.

The following excerpt is from one of my favorite books ever produced, *"This Nonviolent Stuff'll Get You Killed: How Guns Made the Civil Rights Movement Possible,"* by Charles E. Cobb, Jr.

[4]"Whenever we are having a meeting, Raymond told Dennis, C.O. Chinn sits outside with his guns. He won't leave. He says he's here to protect his people. Can you talk to him? So, Dennis recalls: I went outside to talk to him. He's sitting in the back of his truck with a shotgun across his lap and a pistol by his side. I introduced myself, told him about CORE's nonviolent philosophy. He listened. Then, very calmly, he told me: "This is my town, and these are my people. I'm here to protect my people, and even if you don't like this, I'm not going anywhere. So maybe you better leave. I could tell he wasn't a guy for any bull, and I

---

[4] Cobb Jr., Charles E. *"This Nonviolent Stuff'll Get You Killed: How Guns Made the Civil Rights Movement Possible"* (2015), North Carolina: Duke University Press.

could tell he was there to do what he said he was going to do. I didn't argue, "Yes sir," and shook his hand, then walked back into the church thinking he's got his job to do and I've got mine."

Chinn, at this time, was in his early forties, tall, powerfully built, muscular, and dark-skinned. He was an outstanding recruiter for Black voter registration and a very effective speaker. Blacks felt safe in his presence, and his presence was usually all that was needed to give Blacks that extra courage to act and do what was right. His legendary fistfights and shootouts with Klansmen, many of whom were in the sheriff's department and police force, made him the stuff of legends to those who both admired him and hated him--all the more reason to suppress his name for the generations that were not alive to see him and his actions firsthand. He is one of my favorite men of the Black freedom movement. More than an unsung hero, he was, and other men like him were, in fact, why the struggle developed into a movement in the first place. Badass C.O. Chinn of Canton, MS's Madison County. The man, the myth, the legend. A man worthy of remembrance and tribute. Ashe', Ashe', Ashe.'

CHAPTER 15

WHEN EXPRESSING YOURSELF WITH YOUR PEN GETS YOU INTO TROUBLE

*During the height of the second President Bush presidency, affirmative action was a big subject. At the time, many things were being written about its merits and why we, as quote-unquote minorities, needed to praise a President who favored its use. I cut my teeth as a journalist, which is how I responded as a young beat writer and essayist. My views have changed a bit as I have grown older, but my point in including this early writing is to express the power of the pen. This simple article cost me a lot and even earned me a few death threats. The pen is definitely mightier than the sword. Or, at the very least, just as mighty. Write with authority. But write like you play chess.

"I wrote a weekly column in the op-ed section of the Metro Forum Newspaper, a small African American publication in Jackson, Tennessee. This particular entry got me in lots

*of trouble. This experience taught me
two things. First, there is power in
your pen. Secondly, people still read,
even those who despise you."*

- Samuel L. Polk, Jr.

"The case against Affirmative Action"

CIRCA 2002 / The Metro Forum Newspaper, Jackson, TN

The President is getting bolder and bolder in his racism every day. As his military muscles are being flexed all over the world's television programming, he is becoming more and more drunk with the sense of his own power. Even his faith-based initiatives plan is working according to plan. The only place the Bush faith-based initiative program was geared to was the Black Church. But Bush did not tell the Black Church the catch twenty-two for their acceptance of these funds. When the church accepts funds from a governmental agency, it can no longer endorse a political candidate, and we all know that the Black Church blindly supports the Democratic Party candidate no matter who it is or what they are actually saying or not saying on the campaign trail. But by accepting Bush and his administration's money, he has eliminated his competition's advertisement, which is as good as getting direct advertisement and support from the political enemy, direct from the pulpit. Historically, the Black community has looked to the church for direction and guidance from the leadership that speaks directly to the community on a weekly basis.

This will cause uninformed voting decisions or just a no-show on Election Day due to the absence of political instruction. The average Black Church goer will just refrain themselves from participating in a constitutional right that many who talked to them from those very pulpits gave their lives to earn. This may seem strange, but the President's strategy does not offend or bother me. It is a political strategy that is employed to meet an end. Bravo. Political greenness and naivety will get you beaten and kept in a bottom status always. This is what we do not understand.

Yes, affirmative action indeed helped a few Blacks along the way, but as a whole, it really is worthless and of no benefit to us without well-organized political action to enforce it. Sure, it may get an individual a job here and there; what about the millions of Black adults that are not allowed to participate or even know that they can participate? Whenever you see one of us in positions of so-called authority, first make a study of their alliances and their friendship base. If they rise to prominence in government with all the wrongs before mentioned accompaniments, I become very suspicious. Look at Clarence Thomas! affirmative action helped him get to his position professionally, but why not Judge Joe Brown? The difference is who has whose best interests at heart.

My point is that affirmative action is only a quota. A NIGGER HERE, A NIGGER THERE, A BLACK WOMAN HERE, ONE THERE. But who are they really and outside of looking like us, who sent them? A female minority can kill two birds with one stone if they are making all of our decisions for us politically. Condoleezza Rice, for example, would Bush allow Angela Davis to work that closely with the White House? Davis is just as qualified, possibly even more so, but whose best interest does she have at heart and in mind?

I'm simply saying that affirmative action does not benefit us at all unless you are willing to participate in all levels of the political arena. By all levels, I mean accepting financial contributions from people or contributions that totally contradict the reason that people who believe in you are sending you there in the first place. The interests of those that are counting on you will not be allowed to supersede those of the people who now control you. One Black person being guaranteed a spot may sound good on its surface, but if we are not putting ourselves in positions to decide who that one will be, it's inevitable to be one that has their best interests at heart rather than ours. Yes, they will pick a Clarence Thomas to do the job, and what good does he mean to the African American community even though he came from it? Even though we are as good as we have become at the law, they make the law and change it whenever we take advantage of it. We do not need charity; we need true and proper reparations just as others have received that went through much less for much less of a time than us.

We need a political revolution. A 180-degree change in the way we do business politically. Creating our own companies on the same playing field as our counterparts will eliminate the need for charity, such as affirmative (non) action. The steps taken to get the government to see the need for affirmative action were a step in the right direction. But once gained, we celebrated like the war was over and lost our war footing. If you call being able to eat at a lunch counter alongside your former slave master a victory, it was no more ridiculous for a slave to think since he was now working in the house that he had made it because he had started in the fields. If you are a butler working for a poor man, you will be poor. If you are a butler working for a rich man, you will be better off, but you will still be a butler. As America grows in wealth, so will her butlers, but if the butler ever loses sight that it is still the subservient position, then the brainwashing has been complete.

To be asked or forced to participate in a capitalistic society without capital or the tools to produce real capital is a crime. Simply put, the enemy will not allow you to take jobs away from his people, and you are a fool if you do not recognize this by now. We are in our own way. The segregation that we fought so hard to destroy is, in fact, the reason we were better off back in the day. We had no choice but to support our own. The minute it ended, all of our schools, hospitals, banks, theaters, stores, etc., went down rapidly.

Simply put, affirmative action has helped everyone but who it was intended to help. Some of those who have advanced because of it now want to see to its end. Historically Black Colleges are maybe the best example of this. Progress means leaving the institutions that got you to this point for those who have historically denied you access because of your skin color. Student populations dwindled, top-tier athletes left in droves, and so did some of our best minds serving as coaches. Is affirmative action needed when you organize with your own, do business with your own, and hire and work with your own? I humbly say no. Can affirmative action be used against you in your own institutions by the oppressor class seeking minority grants and scholarships? I say that it already has? My words may offend some, and that is certainly not my intention. Personal offense aside, can you deny the validity of my points presented here. With all of the blind praise for affirmative action and even President Bush's Faith-based initiatives, which will have deep underlying consequences for the Black church, I felt it necessary to offer an opposing viewpoint.

Affirmative action was an attempt to right a wrong. Maybe even designed with the best of intentions. Need I remind the reader that the road to Hell is sometimes paved with good intentions? Just another way of looking at a social construct of seemingly helpful merit. Let us continue to reason together in the spirit of our ancestors. Ashe

CHAPTER 16

THE PIONEER, THE HALL OF FAMER, AND A REPRESENTATION SORELY MISSED

> *"Until I saw people who looked like me, doing the things I wanted to, I wasn't sure it was a possibility. Seeing Whoopi Goldberg and Oprah in The Color Purple, it dawned on me: 'Oh, I could be an actress!' We plant the seed of possibility."*

When I was nine years old, an exciting moment took place in the Polk household. We got cable television. I had listened to friends talk about watching things that sound so amazing to me that I would have done anything to have that experience each and every night sitting in front of the television. A man came over one Saturday morning during the fall of that year and started fiddling with our T.V. I thought maybe he was repairing it, I really had no idea what he was doing and paying it no attention I went outside to play, mess around and see what I could get into. The smell of my mother cooking breakfast drew my attention back inside as the strange man was leaving. After he walked out of the door and was gone, my father informed my sister and me that we now had cable. Oh man, my head swelled with excitement as I contemplated the possibilities. I grabbed the remote and discovered "The Super Friends" and various other Saturday morning cartoons that I had only heard about from classmates and neighborhood friends. As my father took the remote from me, which was a signal that it was time to do some Saturday morning yard work, my mind was still on those new cartoons and cable televised movies I had never seen.

Once we wrapped things up, it was well into the afternoon, and I ran inside and grabbed the remote once more. Flicking through the seemingly endless number of channels, only really about 50 of them, but before that day, we only had 5. WLBT, WJTV, WDBD Fox 40 and PBS. I thought it could never get any better than this. I was wrong.

Jackson State must have had an open date that night because we did not go to a home game or observe a tradition within my house that my father and I partook in whenever the Tigers were on the road. Listening to the JSU football game via the radio broadcast, hosted by brilliant radio announcer and voice of the Tigers Bob Carpenter while my father and I enjoyed boiled peanuts and coke floats. This night found us home, and I was on the hunt to watch something new and boy did I find it. Flipping through the channels, I came upon a football game. But not the kind I had seen before on television. This was way too familiar, and without a doubt, I immediately recognized one of the teams. I had seen them many times before. It was the SWAC's own Southern University Jaguars. I heard the bands blowing and jumped up off the couch and slid onto the floor as nine years old's tend to do. The other team was the Delaware State University Hornets. My Dad was in the kitchen, and I said, Dad did you know there was a Black College in Delaware? I then asked Dad did he know they showed Black college games on T.V. He broke down to me what Black Entertainment Television (BET) was and what it was all about. I then remembered seeing those huge black and gold BET signs inside the Vet when the Tigers played from time to time. I was beside myself. This cable thing was going to be better than I thought.

The voice covering the game was an eloquent, articulate, and deep voice belonging to one Charlie Neal "The Voice of Black College Sports." The second voice was a college classmate of my father's, Hall of Famer, and former superstar cornerback and kick returner Lem Barney as the color commentator. They were phenomenal together. It was funny, insightful, and really made me proud the way they represented this authentic and super black form of college football that I would never have guessed had ever been televised. From that moment on, I watched a Black College Football matchup on BET every Saturday that we were not attending a Tigers game in town or on the road.

Imagine the brevity of this use of a Black media platform. It was genius and so very needed. BET had provided scores of African American parents and families a way to watch their sons play. This was a Godsend to many who would have never been able to afford to watch their child fulfill a lifelong dream of playing college ball. I discovered for a while and learned of new HBCUs I had previously not known even existed. The broadcast would give all of the Saturday's Black College football scores, National and conference rankings and even showed portions of both bands halftime field shows. Some of my fondest memories regarding televised football centered on BET Black College football. How many kids growing up in the North, out West, and the Midwest became familiar with HBCUs from this cultural expression of media representation? So popular during this time, I have even heard that BET's prime time games hurt the big names on regular network television so badly, that is one of the reasons the telecast disappeared.

I wish there was a way we could recreate this moment again for so many young African American people today. Yes, HBCUs are on television today, "but it ain't BET STYLE." It is not the way Charlie Neal and Lem Barney did it. They did it in an unapologetically Black way. A respect of the cultural expressions that mainstream telecasts cut short or show no airtime. One thing that a person learns is that change is the only constant thing in this universe, and nothing stays the same for very long. Honestly, I know this is a much different world and social dynamic from the one I grew up in, but that does not mean that these memories should ever die. People we see on television today, black people, many of whom are there only because they saw a Charlie Neal and a Lem Barney doing what they would learn they wanted to do as well. Not that they had not seen it before in the form of an Al Michaels or a Keith Jackson, but it's just different when they look like you do. Ways of knowing.

CHAPTER 17

THE 'SIP

"My passion comes from the things that have historically happened to Black people in Mississippi."

\- David Banner

Hartman Turnbow, a hero of the Mississippi freedom struggle, was a righteous warrior. When scary tactics were used against Blacks attempting to register to vote in the Delta, Hartman was the first to raise his hand when the group was asked in a most intimidating way. Hartman raised his hand and famously responded, "I'll be first." Then, in just as threatening a manner, he was asked by white officials, "What's your name, boy!" Again, without hesitation, Hartman responded, "Hartman, Hartman Turnbow." Later that night, the Klan attempted to burn the Turnbow home down with him and his family in it asleep. Hartman heard the noise, grabbed his gun, and began to fire at the men, undoubtedly trying to send a message to him that his behavior earlier that day would not be tolerated in the state. Hartman struck several, killing at least one who later died as a result of his injuries. Hartman later responded that he was not trying to be "non-violent," "I was just trying to protect my family." Hartman later was charged with attempting to burn down his own home for attention. In a meeting with Rev. Dr. Martin Luther King, Jr., Hartman told the Civil Rights powerhouse that "This non-violent stuff is no good. Not in Mississippi. This non-violent shit will get you killed."

Unlike most places engaged in Civil Rights activities, Mississippi did not take hold of the idea of non-violence as a strategy or way of life. This phenomenon has early origins in the state. It was a spirit to fight back at all costs against the oppressor that never died out in the Africans and people of African descent, enslaved throughout the State of Mississippi. The French were the responsible party of criminals that brought the first Africans held in the bonds of slavery to the State of Mississippi. Their destination was Natchez, Mississippi. Those first groups of Africans gave the French enslavers hell on the ships and land once they had docked. There was never a time when Black Mississippi did not resist white domination over their lives and natural right to self-determination.

As evidence of this, the earliest of these efforts to resist is documented as having occurred in the year 1729. The initial contact between the Natchez Indians and the Africans brought there against their will formed into a mutual partnership. The Natchez Indians were engaged in their own resistance efforts against the British. The Natchez Indians started to reach out to the Africans, and with a mutual enemy, they soon became close. They developed a closeness similar to the kind two men of different races and backgrounds forge while stuck in a foxhole during the war. The Natchez Indians recruited many of these Africans, and they formed a unit primed and ready to take action against the French and the British. In the year 1729, this unit of Black men and Redmen comrades in a struggle for freedom staged a revolt of epic size and scope. So aggressive that it would shape and solidify the type of cruelty that would be used to not only eliminate the Natchez Indians but punish Africans in the state for decades and decades afterward.

This righteous revolt would end in the killing of 230 people. The full might of white supremacy was brought against all that participated and many that had not. This resulted in an even crueler form of slavery that the State of Mississippi became famous for. The Natchez Indians, a close ally of the Africans brought forcibly into their lands, were punished to no end. Many of the Natchez were sold into slavery and taken to the Caribbean for breaking and selling to other parts of the western hemisphere. An old blues song, "Natchez Burning," sung by Mississippi blues legend Howling Wolf, aka Chester Author, was a haunting song that was a way of knowing that is priceless in terms of ancestor veneration and ways of remembering. However, it was noted that howling Wolf was singing about a more recent act of violence perpetrated by white vigilante groups in the town of Natchez.

In 1857, a white overseer of enslaved persons was killed for his cruelty by Cedar Grove Plantation Slaves in the southeastern region of Natchez, Mississippi. Many of Cedar Grove's slave population were tortured and killed, while others were forced to confess and then killed. But it never killed Black Mississippi's will to fight back and keep fighting until victory was won.

Jackson, Mississippi, the place of my birth, got its name from a man that this country considers a national treasure and hero of most admirable quality. Using intellectual honesty and an African-centered thought process will make the correct analysis that he was an evil man, a murderer, kidnapper, rapist, and lunatic. The Capital

City of Jackson got its name from Tennessean General Andrew Jackson, who would become the 7th President of the United States of America. So thankful that this criminal killed and murdered so many Choctaw Indians in the area, enabling it to be possessed by white Europeans and whites wanting to use this land as farming land to be worked by the Africans they had enslaved, they called the area Jackson. Jackson, Mississippi. I have always believed that the continued fight for freedom that has been waged here in this land by Africans will eventually end in victory. We don't turn no Jaws here. And we carry on the fight.

C.O. Chinn, E.W. Steptoe, Fannie Lou Hammer, Medgar, and Charles Evers, Vernon Dahmer, Hartman Turnbow, Amzie Moore, Chokwe Lumumba, Skip Robinson, Rudy Shields, James Meredith, Luella Hazelwood, and Bishop Charles Tucker who once said, "Any Negro or white has the right to defend himself with arms. Any man who didn't ought to take off his pants and wear a skirt." Add your own names to this list and call the roll aloud. Say their names, learn about them, and study their lives. Malcolm X said that history is the subject best suited to reward our research. Ancestor veneration and remembering those who have come this way before you are vital for our success as a people. I wake up every morning with two goals for my day. The first is to learn at least one thing about my people that I did not know the day before. The second thing is to teach someone something that they did not previously know. I haven't failed to accomplish at least one of these goals in the last twenty-five years. Mostly, I accomplish both each day, and it is the reason I rise in the morning. It never gets old; it never gets boring. That's my mission, and my attitude is like that of the great

David "Wavee Dave" Chambers; it's a divine mission. And I wish you would disturb me on my post. Uhuru.

CHAPTER 18

COFO & TAKING CONTROL OF OUR OWN NARRATIVES

> *"I think some of the most significant things happen in history when you get the right people in the right place at the right time, and I think that's what we are."*
>
> -Mayor Chokwe Lumumba

During the football season of 1961, Jackson State claimed outright possession of the SWAC Championship. The Tigers would lose to Jake Gaither's Florida A&M Rattlers at the end of the season, securing that the Rattlers would be recognized as the Black College National Champions in 1961. The following season in 1962, the Tigers of Jackson State, under the leadership of "Big" John Merritt, would return with a 10-1 record, again facing the Gaither led Rattlers of FAMU, this time defeating them and becoming the Black College National Champions. Quarterback Ron Curry and receiver Willie Richardson put on a show in the Tigers' 22-6 victory over the Rattlers. Richardson and Curry would later be inducted into the College Football Hall of Fame. Richardson would become a voice I loved listening to on the Tiger's game day radio broadcasts as the color commentator following a stellar professional football career playing with the Baltimore Colts. Soon another Mississippi native would dump conventional wisdom on its head by transferring from

Jackson State to 'Ole Miss (University of Mississippi), enrolling as its first student of African heritage, getting him shot in an attempted assassination during his one-man march against fear. His name was James Meredith.

The level of fervor for Black history has increased in recent decades, but it is primarily the same as it was when I was coming up. Although I am thankful for those who attempt to make a difference, the presentation can be dry and watered down most of the time from a national format. For those having heard the presentation the previous year, the next year, it gets old. I feel this is due to the packaging of information about our heroes, and their stories are presented in such a way as not to anger those who put us in this situation in the first place. The same few names are talked about repeatedly, and although these names are certainly worthy of tribute, they are not the only ones, and in some cases, they are not even the best examples of our best doing their best. What I feel can be even more helpful in these efforts is to localize the history of the people living in an area to touch them with histories and stories of men and women that they can touch, feel and share a dialogue with people who actually knew them. This will undoubtedly give rise to names, subjects, and events that the student has never heard of. This is good because now the hearer of this information is now learning and not being bored to death just hearing the same spill each and every year. In fact, there is enough history and valuable information to tell these stories every day of the year and never really scratch the surface.

Mississippi was a hotbed of social and civil political activity. Not much has changed in that regard over the decades. Outside of certain circles of activity, these happenings, struggles, losses, victories, miracles, and fights had and will go unnoticed and unknown even to those who have and will benefit from the brave men and women who engaged in them.

Mississippi was now becoming packed with organizational activity and mobilization as the 1950s turned into the 1960s. The Congress of Racial Equality (CORE), The National Association for The Advancement of Colored People (NAACP), The Southern Christian Leadership Conference (SCLC), and The Student Nonviolent Coordinating Committee (SNCC), just to name a few, were working hard in the State against the racist and oppressive forces fighting desperately to maintain their way of life first established in the days of chattel slavery. In an effort to organize these groups in the collective spirit of work and responsibility, another organization was given birth into the fight for justice in Mississippi.

The year was 1961. The location was 107 John R. Lynch Street just at the edge of the Jackson State University campus and nestled within the Black business district of Jackson teaming with thriving Black businesses ranging for barbershops, restaurants, cafes, cleaners, dry cleaners, drugstores, and even a movie theater that catered to all Black audiences. Another legacy that needs to be preserved is the story of Farish Street and the shining example of Black business acumen and excellence it provided the Black community in Jackson for so long. Nevertheless, during the year 1961, just a stone's throw from J-State was an organization created to help organize the rest. It was called The Council of Confederated Organizations (COFO). Lynch Street was home to the campus of JSU and the Prince Hall Masonic Temple, where the offices of Medgar Evers, then Field Secretary for the NAACP. Lynch Street also was host to all sorts of other political activity and revolutionary advancement. Just to add some historical context, John R. Lynch was an African American man born into slavery on or about September 10, 1847, in Vidalia, Louisiana. That very man rose to be appointed Justice of the Peace in 1869, and later that year elected successfully as the first Black to hold office in the Mississippi State House, re-elected, and also elected as Speaker of the Mississippi State House. Just some context because the Street name often congers up other feelings whenever the Lynch name is mentioned so close to an HBCU. Just a proactive explanation of how Lynch Street got its name and whom it got it from.

Although not around for very long, COFO brought into fruition major things that have stood the test of time. The Mississippi Freedom Democratic Party (MFDP) was brought into existence as an outgrowth of other activities, partnerships, and interests. The Mississippi Freedom Democratic Party gave Mrs. Fannie Lou Hammer a national stage and platform. COFO also was the creator of the Mississippi Freedom Summer Project in 1964. These activities certainly increased the level of barbarity that white citizens expressed their disapproval, in the form of Church bombings and fires, murders, and denials of political rights to Blacks, such as voter registration and voting periods. Never deterred these organizations being powered by HBCU students from Jackson State, nearby Tougaloo College, Alcorn State, Mississippi Valley State, Rust College, and Hinds-Utica as foot soldiers carried on the fight and never gave in to actions of Jim Crow Mississippi in the death throes of defeat. On the campus of JSU was created The COFO Center to preserve its memory and the memory of the greater Civil Rights struggle in the State.

These are just a few examples of stories that should be localized on a global scale to teach our people about themselves and what they have done right in their own backyards and vice versa. This will never get boring, and the information, well, will never run out.

CONCLUSION

MISSISSIPPI's THREE SWAC MEMBER INSTITUTIONS / WAYS OF KNOWING / WAYS OF REMEMBERING

"Success is to be measured not so much by the position that one has reached in life as by the obstacles which he has overcome."

-Booker T. Washington

Alcorn State University is significant in history for several reasons, one of which is that it is this country's first Black land grant college founded in 1871 in Lorman, Mississippi. From the years of 1871-1882, Hiram Rhodes Revels served as the President of Alcorn State. Hiram Rhodes Revels was also the first African American to serve in either the United States House or the United States Senate. Alcorn Agricultural and Mechanical College's name was changed to Alcorn State University in 1974. The 'Corn's colors are purple and gold, and the ASU mascot is the Brave. Motto / "Where Knowledge and Character Matter." Alcorn State University joined the Southwestern Athletic Conference (SWAC) in 1962.

On October 23, 1877, Jackson State University developed out of what was called Natchez Seminary in Natchez, Mississippi. The American Baptist Home Mission Society of New York was the responsible party credited with the school's establishment. In 1883, the campus moved to the capital city of Jackson in a location that now serves as the campus of Millsaps College. In 1943, The

Baptist Society took away its financial support, and the school became a public institution which in 1940 was renamed Mississippi Negro Training School. In 1944, the name was changed to Jackson College for teachers. It became Jackson State College and finally Jackson State University in 1974. JSU'S mascot is the Bengal Tiger, and the school's colors are navy blue and white. But for those in my era, that "Gorden Red" is a must, or it just doesn't look right. Motto / "Challenging Minds, Changing Lives." Jackson State University joined the Southwestern Athletic Conference (SWAC) in 1958.

Mississippi Valley State University was established in 1950 as Mississippi Vocational College in response to legal public segregation officially coming to an end by the Mississippi legislature in an effort to keep as many young Black students from attempting to gain admittance into Mississippi's white institutions of higher learning. It is located in Itta Bena, Mississippi. By 1964, the school's name was changed to Mississippi Valley State College. And in 1974, it was named Mississippi Valley State University. School colors are forest green, red and white. The mascot of MVSU is the Delta Devil. Motto / "Life for Service." Mississippi Valley State University joined the Southwestern Athletic Conference (SWAC) in 1968.

Bitter rivals of the highest regard, these great Black institutions are legacies to the spirit and progress and fight within the descendants of Africa currently living in the state or born and raised here. Although the rivalries are the stuff of legends, this indeed is a big family in which brotherhood is both a necessity and a pleasure to live.

Words have power and can be uttered in a harmful or helpful way. I often use two words in my regular vocabulary: the Swahili word Uhuru and the Yoruba word Ashe. Uhuru simply means freedom. Freedom is something that I desperately wish for people of African descent throughout the African Diaspora. Freedom is something that has been deprived and forcefully taken from people of African descent and our institutions for far too long.

Ashe, more of a concept of philosophical origins brought into the universe by the Yoruba people, mainly of Nigeria. Ashe is the power to make things happen and the power to change the things that need to be changed. The power of Ashe can only be given out by Olodumare. Ashe gives your songs, prayers, the activity of your hands, the spirit needed to create good, and the excellence to take care of business and get on with the work of getting free. To anyone who has taken the time to read this humble work, I am with Uhuru and Ashe in observance of our ancestors. And the belief that meshing together the history and stories of growing up Black in Mississippi with a glorious past where we made something out of nothing in a quest to educate ourselves in a country that made the fundamental act of learning to read and write an illegal one. The Black College Football Cultural Framework meshed with African-centered thought expressed in the pages of "I ONLY HAVE AN HOUR" is my way of remembering. My way of knowing.

- Samuel L. Polk, Jr.

FURTHER READING LIST

Dressman, Denny. *Eddie Robinson "he was the Martin Luther King of football."* Paros Press, 2010

Lock, Carlos. *Black College Football "The Game That Time Forgot."* Bardolf & Company, 2020

James, Jr., Dr. Jimmie, and James Arthur. *The Legendary Voice Of The Sonic Boom Of The South.* Dorrance Publishing Company, 2017

Wilson, Roosevelt. *Jake Gaither "Agile, Mobile, Hostile.* Published by Roosevelt Wilson, 2017

Hurd, Michael. *"Collie J" Grambling's Man With The Golden Pen.* St. Johann Press, 2007

Fink, Rob. *Football At Historically Black Colleges And Universities In Texas.* Texas A&M University Press, 2019

Freedman, Samuel G. *Breaking The Line "The Season In Black College Football That Transformed The Sport And Changed The Course Of Civil Rights."* Simon & Schuster, 2013

Posey, Josephine McCann. *Against Great Odds "The History Of Alcorn State University."* University Of Mississippi Press, 1994

Cooke, Anna L. *Lane College: Its Heritage And Outreach 1882 - 1982.* Lane College, 1987

Stodghill, Rod. *Where Everybody Looks Like Me "At The Crossroads Of America's Black Colleges And Culture.* Harper Collins, 2015

Akuno, Kali & Nangwaya, Ajamu, Cooperation Jackson. *Jackson Rising "The Struggle For Economic Democracy*

And Black Self-Determination In Jackson, Mississippi." Daraja Press, 2017

Umoja, Akinyele Omowale. *We Will Shoot Back "Armed Resistance In The Mississippi Freedom Movement."* New York University Press, 2013

Hill, Lance. *The Deacons For Defense "Armed Resistance And The Civil Rights Movement."* The University Of North Carolina Press, 2004

Wendt, Simon. *The Spirit & The Shotgun "Armed Resistance And The Struggle For Civil Rights."* University Press Of Florida, 2007

Cobb Jr., Charles E. *This Nonviolent Stuff'll Get You Killed "How Guns Made The Civil Rights Movement Possible."* Basic Books, 2014

Evers, Charles And Szanton, Andrew. *The Charles Evers Story, Have No Fear "A Black Man's Fight For Respect In America."* John Wiley & Sons, Inc., 1997

Payton, Walter With Yaeger, Don. *The Autobiography Of Walter Payton Never Die Easy.* Villard Books, 2000

Gwin, Minrose. *Writing The Long Civil Rights Movement, Remembering Medgar Evers.* A Sarah Mills Hodge Fund Publication, 2013.

Hurd, Michael. *Black College Football, Revised And Updated Edition, 1892 - 1992, One Hundred Years Of History, Education, And Pride.* The Donning Company /Publishers, 1998

Gaines, Darryl C., And Branson, John M. *Archie "Gunslinger" Cooley, The Making Of A Football Legend.* Opportune Independent Publishing Co., 2019

Lane, Isaac. *The Autobiography Of Bishop Isaac Lane, With A Short History Of The C.M.E.Church In America And Of Methodism.* Printed For The Author Publishing House Of The M.E. Church, South Nashville, Tn, 1916

Edited by Erenrich, Susie. *Freedom Is A Constant Struggle, An Anthology Of Mississippi Civil Rights Movement.* Black Belt Press, 1999

Andrews, Kenneth T. *Freedom Is A Constant Struggle, The Mississippi Civil Movement And Its Legacy.* The University Of Chicago Press, 2004

Biondi, Martha. *The Black Revolution On Campus.* The University Of California Press, 2012

Sojourner, Sue [Lorenzi] with Reltan, Cheryl. *Thunder Of Freedom, Black Leadership And Transformation of 1960's Mississippi.* The University Press Of Kentucky, 2013

Jeffries, Hasan Kwame. *Bloody Lowndes, Civil Rights And Black Power in Alabama's Black Belt.* New York University Press, 2009

Aiello, Thomas. *Bayou Classic, The Grambling - Southern Football Rivalry.* Louisiana State University Press, 2010

Robinson, Eddie with Lapchick, Richard. *Never Before Never Again, The Stirring Autobiography Of Eddie Robinson, The Winningest Coach In The History Of College Football.* St. Martin's Press, 1999

Summerville, James. *Educating Black Doctors, A History Of Meharry Medical College.* The University Of Alabama Press, 1983

Edited By Tyree, Ph.D., Tia C.M. and Cathcart, Christopher D. *HBCU Experience, The Book.* Tyree & Cathcart, 2014

Posey, Josephine McCann. *Alcorn State University And The National Alumni Association (The College History Series).* Arcadia Publishing, 2000

Savage, Phoenix, And Flucker, Turry. *African Americans Of Jackson (Images Of America).* Arcadia Publishing, 2008

Cheeks-Collins, Jennifer E. *Madison County Mississippi (Black America Series).* Arcadia Publishing, 2002

Nossiter, Adam. *Of Long Memory, Mississippi And The Murder Of Medgar Evers.* Da Capo Press, 1994

McClymer, John F. *Mississippi Freedom Summer.* Thompson &Wadsworth, 2004

Willis, John C. *Forgotten Time, The Yazoo-Mississippi Delta after The Civil War.* The University Press Of Virginia, 2000

Newman, Mark. *Divine Agitatore, The Delta Ministry And Civil Rights In Mississippi.* The University Of Georgia Press, 2004

McCord, William. *Mississippi: The Long, Hot Summer.* University Press Of Mississippi-Jackson, 2016

Moses, Robert P. And Cobb, Jr., Charles E. *Radical Equations, Civil Right From Mississippi To The Algebra Project.* Beacon Press, 2001

Williams, Myrlie Evers-Williams & Marable, Manning. *The Autobiography Of Medgar Evers, A Hero's Life, And*

Legacy Revealed Through His Writings, Letters, And Speeches. Basic Civitas Books, 2005

Beito, Linda Royster And Beito, David T. *Black Maverick, T.R.M. Howard's Fight For Civil Rights And Economic Power.* University Of Illinois Press, 2009

Marshall, James P. *Student Activism And Civil Rights In Mississippi, Protest Politics And The Struggle For Racial Justice, 1960-1965.* Louisiana State University Press, 2013

Goudsouzian, Aram. *Down To The Crossroads, Civil Rights, Black Power, And The Meredith March Against Fear.* Farrar, Straus And Giroux-New York, 2014

Dittemer, John. *Local People, The Struggle For Civil Rights In Mississippi.* University Of Illinois Press, 1994

Graham, Lawrence Otis. *The True Story Of America's First Black Dynasty, The Senator And The Socialite.* HarperCollins Publishers, 2006

Vollers, Maryanne. *Ghosts Of Mississippi, The Murder Of Medgar Evers, The Trials Of Byron De La Beckwith, And The Haunting Of The New South.* Little Brown Company, 1995

Morris, Willie. *The Ghosts Of Medgar Evers, The Tale Of Race, Murder, Mississippi, And Hollywood. Random House, 1998*

Berry, Jason. *Amazing Grace With Charles Evers In Mississippi.* Saturday Review Press, 1973

Trillin, Calvin. *Jackson 1964, And Other Dispatches from Fifty Years Of Reporting On Race In America.* Random House, 2016

Walton, Anthony. *Mississippi, An American Journey.* Alfred A. Knopf Inc., 1996

Huffman, Alan. *Mississippi In Africa, The Saga Of The Slaves Of Prospect Hill Plantation And Their Legacy In Liberia Today.* Gotham Books, 2004

Lomax, Alan. *The Land Where The Blues Began.* A Delta Book Published By Dell Publishing Group, Inc., 1993

REFERENCES

Dressman, Denny. "Eddie Robinson...he was the Martin Luther King of football" (2010). Denver: Comserv Books.

Millburn, Claire. "An Oral History of Marching Band Traditions of Historically Black Colleges & Universities" (2019), LSU Master's Thesis, 4906.

Umosa, Akinyele Onowale"We Will Shoot Back Armed Resistance in The Mississippi Freedom Movement" (2013) New York: New York University Press.

Cobb Jr., Charles E. "This Nonviolent Stuff'll Get You Killed: How Guns Made The Civil Rights Movement Possible" (2015) North Carolina: Duke University Press.

Made in the USA
Las Vegas, NV
24 July 2021